Taft, Holmes,
and the 1920s Court

Taft, Holmes, and the 1920s Court

An Appraisal

David H. Burton

Madison • Teaneck
Fairleigh Dickinson University Press
London: Associated University Presses

Associated University Presses
440 Forsgate Drive
Cranbury, NJ 08512

Associated University Presses
16 Barter Street
London WC1A 2AH, England

Associated University Presses
P.O. Box 338, Port Credit
Mississauga, Ontario
Canada L5G 4L8

The paper used in this publication meets the requirements
of the American National Standard for Permanence of Paper
for Printed Library Materials Z39.48-1984.

Library of Congress Cataloging-in-Publication Data

Burton, David Henry, 1925–
    Taft, Holmes, and the 1920s court : an appraisal / David H. Burton.
        p.   cm.
    Includes bibliographical references (p.   ) and index.
    ISBN 0-8386-3768-X (alk. paper)
    1. Taft, William H. (William Howard), 1857–1930.   2. Holmes, Oliver Wendell, 1841–1935.   3. Judges—United States—Biography. 4. United States.   Supreme Court—Biography.   I. Title.
KF8744.B874   1998
347.73'26—dc21
[B]   98-10012
                                                                 CIP

PRINTED IN THE UNITED STATES OF AMERICA

For
John S. Monagan
and
Morton S. Jaffe
Craftsmen of the Law
Keepers of the Flame

Contents

Preface

In 1921, WILLIAM HOWARD TAFT BECAME CHIEF JUSTICE OF THE UNITED States. One of his fellow justices, a veteran of nearly twenty years on the bench, was Oliver Wendell Holmes, Jr. Despite differences in judging the law the two became good friends, whose mutual esteem was one of the features of the 1920s court. For both men their justiceships were the capstones of their careers in public service from which they gained immediate personal satisfaction as well as national acclaim.

Historians and biographers have yet to treat Taft and Holmes as cut from the same bolt of cloth. Ordinarily, Taft is remembered as both a judicial conservative and a court activist. For his part, Holmes has been celebrated as a court liberal and an advocate of judicial restraint. Such characterizations are accurate enough, as far as they go. Taft, however, gave clear indications that legal realism had a place in American jurisprudence, and from time to time Holmes was heard to speak in less than liberal tones.

This study delivers more than its title appears to promise, yet the title remains appropriate. It is an account not only of the decade of their common court membership but an explanation as well how Taft and Holmes arrived at the summit of their public vocations. It reveals their common heritage and traces their divergence in jurisprudential matters. They derived from like backgrounds in family and fortune and grew to manhood when scientific materialism was the persuasive philosophy. It was as knights-errant they entered the legal lists, bent on doing justice. Yet in the fulness of their years there had emerged two justices and two different meanings which they gave to the great law, the Constitution.

What was it about them—natural or instinctive, studied or acquired—that denied them a common philosophy of the law? And, when evidence can be advanced to explain their diversity, were Taft and Holmes merely representative of the variations common to individual reactions to and interpretations of the intellectual forces at work in society? Or were they competing symbols for the spirit of an age?

The method employed to get at these and other questions is dual

9

quasi-biographical. Much biographical detail is presumed. Life experiences are treated to the extent necessary to convey comparative and contrasting elements in their growth and development, in their thought and work. Take, for example, their educational careers at Yale and Harvard, making allowances for the sixteen years' difference in their ages. Or again, consider the early Washington days when they were important men in the capital of the emerging American colossus. Can Taft's entry into political life offer some indication of his later judicial opinions, in contrast to Holmes's sequestered years on the high court?

There are paths to follow, friendships to be evaluated (including their own), and writings to be examined as their lives resembled one another, running on parallel but widely divided lines that finally merged in the 1920s court. There a final contest between opposing visions took place, one with unanticipated results. Analysis of their work on the 1920s court, building up from the early chapters, promises to render the results more understandable.

In prefacing this study, it is important to note that Taft and Holmes are treated as important men of the law, and beyond that, as equally important public servants. Although Holmes was senior in age, Taft had attained the two highest offices provided in the Constitution. By reference to formalities, Taft, as president and later as chief justice, outranked Holmes by a goodly measure. In contrast, Holmes enjoys the greater historical reputation without impugning Taft's ability as a legal thinker. By cutting across the grain—in other words, by writing about Taft and Holmes rather than Holmes and Taft, and given the aim of this study (namely, an analysis of the 1920s court, a Taft court)—I am asking the reader to put aside the image of Holmes as the grand panjandrum of the law. In fact, to do so requires little more than reading history and biography forward, not backward, always the best way to proceed. The pertinence of this caveat is made more explicit by pointing out in the year Taft was Solicitor General of the United States, Holmes was best known for his scholarly book, *The Common Law*, not for his interpretations of the Constitution of the United States. Or again, when Holmes was a member of the Supreme Judicial Court of Massachusetts, William Howard Taft was serving as a federal circuit court judge in Ohio. The reader must be reminded of such considerations to explain, if not to justify, the emphases that obtain in approaching Taft, Holmes and the 1920s court.

Both individuals and institutions merit thanks for helping me in the research and writing of this book. Saint Joseph's University has extended support in various ways and the Earhart Foundation provided a generous and timely grant, thereby aiding in the completion of the work. My colleague, Professor Graham Lee, has been a wise counselor and generous friend to the project from its very inception. Chris Dixon of the staff of Drexel Library, Saint Joseph's University, has been a ready and reliable source of advice and help. I allow the dedication of this volume to speak to the role played by two esteemed men of letters and the law.

Taft, Holmes,
and the 1920s Court

Introduction

AT THE MIDPOINT OF THE NINETEENTH CENTURY, THE AMERICAN MIND was basically traditional. The values that society honored and lived by looked mostly to the past. This was the intellectual and moral milieu into which William Howard Taft and Oliver Wendell Holmes were born. If their own particular home environment was not as typical as the conventions of the time dictated nevertheless the larger world in which they were to move, and take exception to, must be identified and grounded in inherited and long-maintained principles. Taft and Holmes were of that generation which was to challenge old ways of thinking and acting as they helped in singular fashion to recast the American outlook. Because the changes brought about by the scientific revolution were not all-inclusive, because there occurred a synthesis in which old ideas were wedded to new ideas to produce new truth, some account of the nature of those old ideas is appropriate. By touching on American religion and philosophy, law and government, and economic theory and practice, the adaptations made by both Taft and Holmes may be more readily understood.

A reminder of where America stood in 1850 is my purpose in this introduction. The most critical development in American thought in the last third of the nineteenth century, the formative decades for Taft and Holmes as men of the law, was that supernaturalism was undercut by new findings in the physical and natural sciences. The dramatic and seemingly irresistible triumph of science is warrant enough to direct attention to the traditional elements that were carried forward into the next century. Such ideas, evident in the legal philosophies of Taft and Holmes, would influence many of their most important court opinions.

In the first half of the nineteenth century the spirit of traditionalism in American religion was especially prominent. At its core was supernaturalism. American Protestant Christianity was based on a literal interpretation of the Biblical narration, an emphasis on the reality of a God of justice and mercy, belief in Christ as a personal savior, and the undoubted certainty of individual survival after death to enjoy reward

15

or punishment commensurate with one's earthly conduct. The religious message remained substantially what it had been since the Reformation, despite a drastic alteration in church organization and an enlargement of emotional content, both of which occurred in America in the eighteenth and nineteenth centuries. In the words of one spokesman for traditional theology, belief was "autochthonous, aboriginal, self-sprung from the Bible, or through the Bible from the skies." Its purpose was a re-creation of the spirit and hope of primitive Christianity, to be accomplished by the methods of revivalism. For example, Charles Grandison Finney, the most renowned evangelical preacher in the pre-Civil War era, declared his independence of learning, along with an avowal of faith in the Bible literally taken. Refusing the opportunity to study at the theological seminary in Princeton, Finney declared that, to come to a knowledge of the teachings of Christ, he relied on nothing "except my Bible and what I found there."[1] Finney was not a strict Calvinist, however; questioning parts of the Westminster Confession, he appealed more to faith than to theology.

The evangelical spirit, with its intense emotional appeal fashioned in the style of the Great Awakening, tended to confirm the traditional message of salvation. It was undoubtedly anti–intellectual, and on that score vulnerable, when it came into open conflict with science and the philosophies derived from scientific postulates. The simple emotionalism of revivalist preaching proved an easy mark for anyone who chose to pillory it as unlearned. Nevertheless, the traditional, supernatural theology it stood for continued to persuade a decided majority of Americans down to the Civil War.

The kinship of religion and philosophy that remained a feature of the American mind till mid-century predetermined the traditionalism of philosophy as a discipline. American philosophy was by no means innocent of the influences of the Enlightenment and in virtue of these influences it enjoyed contact with and stimulation from leading European thinkers. The Enlightenment, in America as in Europe, represented a kind of marriage of rational thought with religion and morality; thus, it was logical enough to use rational principles to provide a philosophical groundwork for religious beliefs. Although there was much in the Enlightenment that might oppose the orthodoxy of revealed religion, the particular developments in American philosophy, down to the publication of *Origin of Species*, worked to buttress conservative religious doctrine.[2]

In the eighteenth century, Jonathan Edwards undertook to elaborate a Platonic philosophy as a complement to his theological position. Even though no firm line of distinction existed between Edwards's theology and his philosophy, his work marked him as the first great American philosopher. In this regard, Edwards was typical of both Puritanism and the Enlightenment, in that neither was self-consciously "philosophical." But certain emerging philosophical schools tended to cut loose from conventional religion. The strong note of reason in the Unitarianism of William Ellery Channing and Theodore Parker, men whom Esmond Wright has aptly identified as among those "who did not belong," remained without further stimulation until the years of Darwinian dominion.[3]

Meanwhile, traditionalism had found a purposeful ally in Scottish Common Sense philosophy. The Common Sense school restored the grounds for moral and religious certainty in a manner both wholesome and reassuring to its adherents. Among the leading voices of this neo-realism were John Witherspoon and James McCosh, however self-conscious they may have been as thinkers possessed of a predetermined purpose. As McCosh observed in his *Realistic Philosophy*, "the theologians of America have made constant use of philosophic principles in defending their doctrinal positions." The principles he referred to were those of realism, the doctrinal positions, the orthodox Christian faith. Thus he wrote: "if there is to be an American philosophy, it must be Realistic . . . opposed to idealism on one hand and to agnosticism on the other."[4] To McCosh and his colleagues, they had managed a union of reason, as it had developed out of the Enlightenment, an evangelical Christianity that was to dominate the American religious sense well past midcentury.

Few peoples have begun their national history in so formal and auspicious a way as did the Americans of the several states by their Constitution. Their common origin as citizens of self-governing colonies, their experiences as these colonies became states, and the exigencies of their situation in the 1780s all combined to dictate some plan of union for them, though the resulting document was more formidable than could have been predicted. Several factors pertaining to the Constitution and its adoption worked to impart to it, almost at once, unusual possibilities for becoming a bulwark of traditionalism. The troubled times in which the states found themselves at the end of the War for Independence encouraged many to seek a final solution to the difficulties arising from inter-state rivalries and from distress within the states as well. Throughout its labors, the Philadelphia Convention displayed a consciousness of its historic importance in finding such a solution. Political theory current in America taught that men must be free to enter into contracts, giving enduring formality to a particular solution. Once written, the Constitution had to pass the test of ratification by the individual states that would be parties to the contract. A newly constructed frame of government never enjoyed a more authoritative or forceful exposition of its principles and its meaning than did the American Constitution in the *Federalist Papers*. No less a student of government than Thomas Jefferson acknowledged their genius. "Descending from theory to practice," he told fellow Virginian, George Washington, "there is no better book than the *Federalist*."[5] It was as though a New Dispensation and its Commentaries had been born at the same hour. The ingredients the Constitution of the United States possessed for its historic role in tradition were plentiful right from the start.

For those like Washington and his Federalist colleagues, who almost instinctively revered the Constitution and eagerly put it into operation, a feeling of loyalty and attachment to it and the union could not develop too soon. The line of strong presidential advocates of Constitutional majesty ran from Washington to Lincoln. In his "Farewell Address," Washington struck an appropriate and prophetic chord when he reminded his friends and fellow citizens of their adoption of a "Constitution of Government better calculated than your former for an intimate union and for the efficacious management of your common concerns. . . . The Constitution . . . an authentic and explicit act is sacredly obligatory on all of us."[6] The same note of sublimity was sounded by Lincoln on the eve of the Civil War. In his First Inaugural Address he declared: "I hold that, in contemplation of universal law and of the Constitution the Union of these states is perpetual."[7] Presidents from Washington to Lincoln might not have easily agreed on the exact meaning of this or that provision of the Constitution, but, in their own way and time, most of them fostered devotion to the Union, "now and forever, one and inseparable." The cult of the Constitution had been born, to prosper wonderously. Besides presidents, Justices Marshall and Story, as well as senators Clay, Webster, and Benton, and a host of others prominent in the Congress in the early national period, contributed to the mystique of Constitutionalism.

The exertions during the Civil War confirmed the average Northern American's belief in the power and, indeed, the mystery of the Constitution. It became the equivalent of the Southerner's "home and hearth," something worth fighting and dying for. As for Lincoln, he was not

simply politically shrewd when he represented his position as a candidate
for the presidency or his policies in office as aimed, one and all, at
preserving the Constitution and the Union. He was being culturally
honest as well. "Let the history of the Grecian and Italian republics
warn us of our dangers. The national constitution is our last and our
only security. United we stand, divided we fall."[8] These were not the
words of a Civil War leader, but those spoken by Justice Joseph Story
in his *Commentaries on the Constitution of the United States*. The date
was 1833, but the idea contained therein was an American tradition well
established in the age of Jackson and one that Lincoln could draw on.

In profiling the traditionalism of the American mind, its economic
lineaments, though less critical than the religious or the legal-
constitutional, add to the total image. The discipline of theoretical
economics was itself relatively new and limited in appreciation as the
American states entered into a "more perfect Union." On the other
hand, the practical lessons of New World economic activity were so
simple and so obvious to most citizens that theory seemed superfluous.
The Protestant work ethic, when read in combination with the opportunities afforded by the frontier and the generally expanding national
economy, rendered a definition of a "worldly philosophy" less than imperative. A school of clerical economics grew up, prepared to mate
capitalism with the natural order. Francis Wayland, president of Brown
University, wrote a rationale for laissez-faire economic practice called
Elements of Political Economy. Published in 1837, the book went through
several editions before the Civil War, for a total of more than thirty
by 1906. Wayland's views were typical of other clerical economists of
his day.

Clerical economics began by assuming that the capitalist system is a
natural economic system-a happier coincidence for the case of traditionalism is hard to imagine. The limitations of the system arose from either
man's folly or his ignorance, a conclusion which, for men like Wayland,
trained as they were in the ministry, was strikingly like sin. Wayland,
for one, and Francis Bowen of Harvard, for another (in whose course
in political economy, Holmes was expected to recite its lessons), per-
ceived a close analogy between economic activity and morality. In the
view of men, like Wayland and Bowen, property was sacred (another
blow for tradition), and capital represented the accumulation of savings
through the exercise of industry and frugality.[9] The economic system
itself was deemed self-regulating; action by the government was both
unnecessary and unnatural. Clerical economists, however, were not un-

critical defenders of free-swinging laissez-faire with its harmful conse-quences. For example, they considered speculation immoral, while the gloomy views of Malthus found little support among them. The Malthu-sian estimate of things was un-Godly. These clerical economists did not deny that poverty and famine existed, although, for them, such condi-tions in America were so infrequent as to help account for their Godly optimism. Where and when capitalism performed badly, the fault lay in a lack of virtue-industry, frugality, sobriety-on the part of individuals within the system. The net effect was that the teachings of traditional morality were verified anew on economic grounds.

Simultaneously, capitalism received encouragement and approbation under the law, specifically from the political and judicial arms of the national government. As the first Secretary of Treasury, Hamilton early provided direction for growth of a mutually beneficial relationship be-tween capitalism and the government. John Marshall, through his long tenure as chief justice, did further valuable work in the cause of tradi-tionalizing the capitalist system by means of a series of Supreme Court rulings, beginning with *Fletcher* v. *Peck* (1810). Wherever the interests of free enterprise might be served, Marshall's voice was heard, as in the *Dartmouth College Case* (1819), in which he gave his classic definition of a corporation. The legal corporation, so elemental in capitalism, had become part of the enlarging fabric of American traditionalism, abetted, to be sure, by Chief Justice Taney's ruling in the Charles River Bridge case (1837).

In this brief restatement of the traditional qualities of the American mind at the midpoint of the nineteenth century, much that is familiar later is already evident. Science and scientism, to be sure, transmuted, weakened, and even eliminated some of this tradition. Yet traditional essentials remained viable, illustrative of the consensus tendency dis-cernible in many aspects of American life and history. It may be ar-gued—and convincingly—that these elements endured thanks to the efforts of science which rendered them more functional and more appro-priate to changed conditions. Whatever the case, strong elements of conservative thought, firmed into tradition by midcentury, survived the ascendancy of science and therefore continued to stand out as features of the modern American outlook. That they did so can be accounted for both by their utility and by their intrinsic worth—which William Howard Taft and Oliver Wendell Holmes were to take into account as judges and justices.

1

Fellow New Englanders

WHEN TREATING THE LIVES OF THE FAMOUS, IT IS BEST TO BEGIN AT the beginning. So it is with William Howard Taft and Oliver Wendell Holmes, Jr. Their beginnings were buried deep in the soil of New England. Taft's father was a Vermonter who went west. Educated at Yale, he practiced law in Cincinnati and became one of that city's leading citizens. Holmes's family was Boston and Brahmin, with all the trimmings. Even so, it is becoming to provide a reference point or two, drawn from their later lives, to show that the lure of New England continued to exercise a hold on them. Upon retiring from the presidency in 1913, Taft did what was for him the instinctive thing: he became a professor at Yale, his alma mater, settling down in New Haven. Cincinnati was his birthplace, New England was his birthright. The Tafts rented a large house near the university, and the former president was soon a familiar campus figure. At the same time he became active in town affairs and was especially forceful in his insistence that "the Green" remain undisturbed, for he deemed it the center and symbol of the New Haven community. All this had behind it a fondness for the region of his forebears, the first Taft of the American branch of the family having arrived in Massachusetts in the 1670s. A Cincinnati reporter once asked Taft when he planned to return to his Ohio home, to which he replied: "New Haven is good enough for me."[1] In contrast, Holmes was known to internalize his feelings for the New England of his day. Speaking at the 250th anniversary of the founding of the First Church in Cambridge, the date was February 12, 1886, where his grandfather had been minister, he left no doubt of the power of his inheritance. "Even if our mode of expressing our wonder, our awful fear, our abiding trust in the face of life and death and the unfathomable world has changed, yet at this day we New Englanders are still leavened with the Puritan ferment. Our doctrine may have changed, but the cold Puritan passion is still here."[2] The New England conscience, so strangely composed of orthodoxy and

21

tolerance, was at the core of Holmes's being. Two years later, in his opinion in *Heard* v. *Sturgis*, he argued the proposition: "It is only tautologous to say that the law knows nothing of moral rights unless they are also legal rights."[3] Guided by the thought processes of the Puritan divines, Holmes had encased morality in a legal system as a matter of necessity, and thus imparted to the law a moral quality.[4] The love of New England and its ways Taft expressed through his actions, Holmes gave voice to in reflections on life and the law. Despite their common backgrounds and allegiances, this variation was to characterize them as they grew in age and accomplishment. May it not, at the same time, be an intimation of their individual responses to legal issues and to the far-reaching meaning of the Constitution? Taft, the matter-of-fact jurist whose legal writings were not overly concerned with the ultimates of the law, and Holmes, the philosopher-judge for whom law had cosmic as well as a scientific side-these are valid images as the two men sat together on the 1920s court. But they must still be recognized as growing up sons and grandsons of New England.

The England of the seventeenth century gave people reasons enough to seek salvation or fortune—and perhaps both—in the newer England across the sea. Robert, the first Taft in America and a carpenter-farmer, may have been so motivated. Putting down roots in Mindon, a breakaway settlement from Braintree, he soon acquired property, easy enough to do if a man were at all ambitious. He also served as a selectman, which gave him some distinction. One of his sons, Joseph, served as a captain of militia in King Philip's War (1675–76), a struggle that saw many Massachusetts villages laid waste, Mindon among them. Joseph Taft married Elizabeth Emerson, and thus was established a distant relationship between the nineteenth-century Tafts and the "Sage of Concord." According to William Howard Taft, the Emersonian influence on his father was more through books than through blood. Alphonso Taft greatly admired Emerson; though raised a Baptist, he harkened to the teachings of the man Oliver Wendell Holmes, Jr. was to call Uncle Waldo. Emerson's insistence on the worth of every person fostered in the elder Taft a social conscience. Furthermore, legal experience persuaded him that environment can sometimes make lawbreakers and that children especially can become victims of their surroundings. Although this view did not quite amount to a theory of sociological jurisprudence, it did make for a tolerance for those less fortunate in society. As with young Wendell Holmes, William Howard imbibed much of his father's moral convictions, though he proved to be a less definite Emersonian.

The future President was to abandon conventional Protestant theology and become a Unitarian, with all the human values that entailed.

Of the several children born to Elizabeth Emerson Taft, one, Peter, migrated to Vermont, settling in Townsend. Of the next generation, Aaron, who spent some time at the College of New Jersey, in Princeton, was William Howard's grandfather. All in all, the Taft family comes through as one which, over successive generations, acquired property and attained position. It may be significant that no clergymen were included in its ranks—somewhat unusual, considering the number of offspring. Taft men always married New England women. Upon the death of his first wife, Fanny Phelps, whom he had met in Vermont, Alphonso Taft went back to New England in search of another. He found her in Louise Torrey. The Torreys had been in New England as early as the 1640s; by the nineteenth century, the family was highly regarded. On her mother's side, the second Mrs. Taft was a Howard, a family also long settled in the Bay State. The result was that William Howard Taft's ancestry was completely Old Yankee.[5]

Boston was home to Oliver Wendell Holmes, Jr. "I've always lived in Boston," was the terse statement in his college autobiography for the Harvard Alumni Album. In this same sketch is found an apt description of Holmes's family and his sense of it. "All three names," he wrote, "designate families from which I descended. A long pedigree of Olivers and Wendells may be found in the book called 'Memorials of the Dead—King's Chapel Burying Ground.' . . . Some of my ancestors fought in the revolution, among the great grandmothers of the family were Dorothy Quincy and Anne Bradstreet ('the tenth muse'); and so on. . . ."[6] His earliest American forbear was one David Holmes, born in England about 1635, died in Milton, Massachusetts, 1666. Within a brief time, the Holmes family became both plentiful and successful. John Holmes, David's son and a skilled surveyor, built a sawmill and began accumulating land. John's son was "Deacon" Holmes, and after him another David, a revolutionary war officer. Of the next generation there was Rev. Abiel Holmes, a Yale man and clergyman, the father of Dr. Holmes and thus the grandfather of Wendell. The first Wendells were in America by 1640. On this side of the family, he was related to Wendell Phillips, Richard Henry Dana, and William Ellery Channing. Added to this, Dr. Holmes had married a second cousin, Amelia Jackson, giving the impression that the family was at once numerous and distinguished and closely knit. Amelia Jackson's father was a landowner, successful businessman, and judge. If the Holmes side of Wendell's inheritance was

noted for learning with a dash of piety, the Jacksons introduced a preference for the practical. Unlike his contemporary, Henry Adams, Wendell
Holmes grew up in Boston conscious of the place his ancestors had
prepared for him and happy with his future prospects.

In the formation of the mind and spirit of Taft, both his father and
mother worked together to mold the boy into the man. Their contribu-
tions to the process were different and distinct, but a meshing of talents
and wills did much to shape what their son would become. Alphonso
Taft was simultaneously ambitious and self-effacing. In some ways, he
would have been content to live out his life as a Cincinnati judge; yet
he was one of the leaders of the city's cultural and intellectual life. As
a family the Tafts were never estimated to be rich but rather to be
educated and forward-looking. In describing his ancestors, William
Howard's father summed up his own outlook: "men who knew how to
get rich and men who dared to be poor." The senior Taft was politically
active, running twice for governor (he was defeated both times). He
later served briefly in the Grant administration as Secretary of War and
Attorney General. President Arthur named him American Minister to
the Austro-Hungarian Empire and later, and again briefly, as American
Minister to Russia. Whatever he attempted, whether by election or
selection, he did out of service to his country and to his fellow citizens.
Louise Torrey Taft, Alphonso's wife, was well educated, widely read and
traveled, compared to most young ladies of her class and station. She
took her duties as wife and mother with the utmost seriousness. Her
second son, Will, the first child having died in infancy, she acknowledged as her favorite among her five children. Though protective of
him, she nonetheless pushed him forward in school and, for that matter,
in life. Taft responded positively to this mothering. As a grown man
and in public office, he often invited her to accompany him on official
trips. This parenting encouraged him to rely on his family for advice
and support. As a family, the Tafts preferred the Unitarian church, the
least theological denomination. If Unitarianism did not amount to free-
thinking about God and man, it came close and was therefore out of
step with mainstream Protestantism. When approached about assuming
the presidency of Yale in 1899, Taft put his beliefs plainly: "I am a
Unitarian. I believe in God. I do not believe in the divinity of Christ.
And there are many other postulates of the orthodox creed to which I
cannot subscribe. I am not, however, a scoffer at religion but on the
contrary recognize, in the fullest manner, the elevating influence that
it has had and will always have in the history of mankind."[7] Echoes of

Ben Franklin . . . religion has its uses? Shades of Karl Marx, the opium of the people? Hardly. But that position on religion, so forthrightly expressed, brings Taft much closer to Holmes in outlook than their judicial differences might lead one to believe.

The Holmes household, in contrast to that of the Tafts, was dominated by Wendell's father, the celebrated Dr. Holmes. And the contrasts grow more pronounced. Holmes, father and son, were natural rivals. If not a rebellious youth, Wendell was never so sweet of nature and so respectful of his father as young Will. Part of this was due to Dr. Holmes's domineering ways. Strong personalities, the two OWHs were bound to clash. But, as Justice Holmes once told Felix Frankfurter, for all the contention between them, he had to admit that his father had taught him a great deal. Alphonso Taft embraced the tolerant ways of Unitarianism in a quiet and unassuming way; the senior Holmes trumpeted his heterodoxy. He was a free spirit and a free thinker, communicating these values as worthy of emulation by his son. By the time young Holmes had left Harvard College, he had all but given up the old faith, though he retained the cold Puritan passion. Compared to the youthful Taft, Holmes was far more intense in his search for meaning, more introspective, less easily satisfied with answers to the cosmic questions as served up by others. The Tafts read Emerson, Holmes grew up knowing him, first as a guest in his parents' home, then as a friend, adviser, and "moral mentor." In the end, Uncle Waldo's impact on Holmes had less to do with the content of belief and more to do with his methods and his attitude toward old learning, particularly old philosophies. Emerson had denounced the past; Holmes looked to the future. "I regard pretty much everything, especially the greatest things in the way of books as dead in fifty, nowadays twenty years," as he was to tell one friend. "The seeds of thought germinate and produce later seeds. The old structures are remodeled and have electric lights in."[8] Written in 1909, this posture derived from the autocratic Dr. Holmes.

Much or little may be read into the differing display of response exhibited by these sons to their parental upbringing. Certainly Taft did not find authority irksome. The opposite conclusion is the likelier; in his mature years this emerged as a leading character trait. He identified authority with chain of command and was guided by it. As Secretary of War he was ever Theodore Roosevelt's faithful lieutenant, refusing at one juncture to accept a nomination to the Supreme Court out of loyalty to his chief. He expected the same kind of support once he was president. All this goes a long way to explain why he upheld the dismissal of Gifford Pinchot in the controversy over conservation (Pinchot had defied Secretary of Interior Ballinger and thus broke the chain of command). Given this habit of mind, in which authority was the sinew of administrative power, Taft's conservatism in judicial matters is understandable. To Taft, the nation, not the people, was sovereign. Holmes, on the other hand, resisted authority represented at first so grandly by his father, the supreme authority on almost everything. At Harvard he continued to display a lack of reverence for the order of things. On one occasion the faculty voted a public admonition for "repeated gross indecorum in the recitation of Professor Bowen." At another time he provoked the ire of President Felton for disrespectful language that appeared in the *Harvard Magazine*, of which Holmes was an editor.[9] This questioning of authority often concerned intellectual matters; years later, as judge and then justice, this disposition was expressed in several important court opinions, one or more in the 1920s.

Taft, Yale '78, Holmes, Harvard '61—college promoted the intellectual development for both young men, though for Holmes not as it was intended to do. At the same time, there grew within them a more refined sense of life and its meaning. For Taft this amounted to conforming more or less to the Yale pattern; whereas, for Holmes, seemingly at odds with the system, it meant nonconformity. During those years leading to manhood, one important characteristic of the Puritan became more pronounced as these two men learned to become inner-directed as befit their differing temperaments.

The Yale of Taft's day—because of reforms introduced by president Noah Porter, including the establishment of a School of Science, a School of Fine Arts, and a Graduate School—had already taken on the look of a modern university. Accordingly, the faculty was greatly strengthened and Will Taft encountered professors much more in tune with the times than was Holmes's experience at Harvard. William Graham Sumner, appointed to the Yale faculty in 1872, was the teacher Taft recalled most vividly. Fifty years on, he was remembered Sumner as having had "more to do with stimulating my mental activities than any other whom I studied under during my entire course."[10] Little wonder—given Sumner's domineering personality and scholarly dogmatism, as absolute in his judgments as the very people he scorned for closed-mindedness. It is not too much to claim that Sumner intimidated a couple of generations of Yalies, the future president among them. Described as "of large frame and firm head, magnificently bald, somewhat stern of countenance, keen eye and 'iron voice,'" he commanded attention and respect as well as the confidence of his students. As professor of Political Economy, the self-willed Sumner sought to mold his charges in his own ways of thinking about politics and economics. Taft was never to forget his emphasis on property and property rights, although, it must be added, Sumner failed to make his student into a free-trader. The archenemy of protectionism, Sumner, had he lived beyond 1910, would have chided the President for favoring the Payne-Aldrich Tariff and might even have taken some pleasure from Taft's discomfort resulting from the political fallout it caused. To some extent, then, the young Will had come under the spell of another authority figure; as long as he was at Yale, and under the master's eye, he was a disciple of the irrepressible Sumner.

On the whole, Taft fit nicely into the Yale scene. He was studious, abstemious, and popular with his fellows, all of which pleased his father (always a consideration in his behavior). A prizewinner in mathematics in his sophomore year and for composition later on, Taft nevertheless envied those who excelled in declamation. For him, Demosthenes had much more to offer than the ancient poets. Election to Skull and Bones, the elitist society his father had helped found, marked him as a true Old Blue.

Despite his love for alma mater, upon graduation Taft returned home, there to study at the Cincinnati Law School. The year was 1878, and the old ways of learning the law held fast. A half-dozen professors lectured on real property and evidence, on contracts and torts. The case method had no place in the curriculum. These teachers were legal authorities and, because of their knowledge and experience at law, must be listened to. Taft willingly accepted them on those terms; he saw no reason to do otherwise. Of course, the day would come when he had attained high judicial office, as judge and justice; then he would insist on his own authority. Never mind that Taft would seek to impose his will in kindly fashion, for he held firm to his convictions. He believed that those who judged the law were both symbols and spokesmen of authority under law, just as, at the same time, he abominated the use of power *ultra vires*.

As a schoolboy Wendell Holmes learned his Greek and Latin, his mathematics and rhetoric at E. S. Dixwell's Private Latin School. At the same time his inquiring mind, with its strain of skepticism, sharpened and toughened; he was therefore likely to expect that critical inquiry would be part of his Harvard education. Yet Holmes's experience at Harvard may cause one to wonder about its claim of being a leading university, or *the* leading university, which was how it was viewed in Boston. If Harvard had a shaping effect on the mind of Holmes, it was to be a matter of constructive negation, with Wendell resisting, sometimes bitterly, the religious orthodoxy that suffused nearly every course of instruction.

Henry Adams once remarked of the Harvard of the mid-nineteenth century that it "taught little, and that little, ill." A consideration of Holmes's four years there bears Adams out, at least as a general proposition. Harvard thought of itself as having traveled a long way from its foundation in 1636, when it was primarily a seminary for men bound for the clergy, to a seat of general education in the mid-1850s. It was a matter of theory versus reality, however, of pretension contrasted with practice. Congregational church orthodoxy was everywhere. Asa Gray, Holmes's professor of botany, was the only faculty member he encountered who took seriously the recently announced findings of Charles Darwin, and therefore encouraged his students to study Darwinian postulates for what they might suggest about nature, if not society. Elsewhere than in Gray's courses, religious tenets were assumed or directly inculcated. For example, Professor Francis Bowen, in his lectures dealing with the principles of political economy, contended that laissez-faire economics was quite simply the working out of God's plan, and "man cannot interfere with His work without marring it." Holmes's willingness as a judge and a political commentator to throw stones at government authority he later displayed in *Olmstead* v. *United States* (1928). In dissent Holmes commented that it was better that some criminals go free than have the government commit an ignoble act. As he challenged the opinions of his father and the regulations of Harvard officials from President Felton on down, so he was moved in later years to view with suspicion their political counterparts.[11]

The problem Harvard posed for Wendell Holmes was that of authority combined with religion. The books he read and studied, those that absorbed his energies during his college career, are evidence of this. Plato's *Dialogues* was a constant companion. He read Fichte's *Contribution to Mental Philosophy*, contemplated Butler's *Ancient Philosophy* and Cousin's *Modern Philosophy*, and returned again and again to Vaughan's *Hours with the Mystics*. The ongoing struggle to fashion his own peculiar intellectual outlook and the drift of that outlook away from traditional moorings are discernible in his resort to Lowe's volumes, *Comte's Philosophy of the Sciences* and his *Biographical History of Philosophy*. No doubt the latter two books worked to polarize Holmes's thinking on methods of truth-seeking and the possibility of truth-finding, without in the end convincing him of the logical positivist's confident dismissal as irrelevant all that cannot be seen or measured.

Taft was but a youngster when the Civil War erupted; he was to learn of suffering and death, waste and destruction, only vicariously. Years later he would serve as Secretary of War, in peacetime to be sure; and fortunately so, because he was a man of peace. As governor of the Philippines, Taft used his position and power to end the bushwacking war between the army and the Filipino insurrectionaries. He became an important advocate of peace through international cooperation during the last years of his presidency and again in 1918–19 as the world sought peace. His record in this latter regard was admirably nonpartisan. It is well to bear in mind Taft's exposure to war and its aftermath, because it contrasts so tellingly with what Holmes had suffered.

Lincoln's call for volunteers caused Wendell Holmes to enlist even before he had graduated from Harvard. Nonetheless, he was able to receive his degree and shortly thereafter, July 1861, was commissioned a lieutenant of infantry and assigned to the 20th Massachusetts. There was no need on his part to enlist; no special stigma attached to those young men of his generation who did not enlist. Though a great many Harvard men did join the fight, not a few of his social class (the young Henry Adams and William Everett come to mind) did not. Those who shunned military duty were not stirred by the same impulse that stirred Holmes. If his service was an expression of youthful rebellion against parental and institutional authority, his avowed purpose, to help destroy slavery, places the decision in a value setting. Beyond that, we may be sure that Holmes's response to President Lincoln's call for volunteers was patriotic in a direct, ennobling way. Lacking social pressure to join the army, there was a compelling Puritan sense of a duty to be performed. The call to arms came not only from Lincoln but from across the years, across generations of Puritan forbears. Giving an account of his conduct at Balls' Bluff, where he received his first of three wounds, he saw himself as acting "very cool and did my duty I am sure." On another occasion he described himself as "heartily tired and half worn out body and mind by this life; but I believe I am as ready as ever to do my duty." Such evidence bears out the primacy of duty in his set of working values. Even as Holmes was nearing the end of his enlistment and found himself thoroughly whipped by the war, duty remained paramount. "I honestly think that the duty of fighting has ceased for me," he wrote his mother in June of 1864, "ceased because I have laboriously and with much suffering of mind and body earned the right to decide for myself how I can best do my duty to myself, to the country, and if you choose, to God." In like vein he told Charles Eliot Norton about the same time: "If one did not believe this was a crusade in the cause of the whole Christian world, it would be hard to keep the hand to the sword." Such thoughts as these, coming at the end of Holmes's long ordeal as a soldier, lay bare the deep roots of his conviction regarding the war, and much more than the war.[12] This concept of duty was registered in postwar reflections. In an address on Memorial Day, May 30, 1884, Holmes praised the duty he judged his own to be in celebrating the sacrifice of his intimate friend, Henry L. Abbott, killed at Cedar Mountain in August 1862. Of Abbott he said: "He was indeed a Puritan in all his virtues, without the Puritan austerity, for when duty was at an end he who would have been master and leader became the chosen companion in every pleasure a man might honestly enjoy; in action he was sublime."[13] Memories of the war died hard for Wendell Holmes.

At some point in their years to manhood, Taft and Holmes became aware that, willy-nilly, they were children of Puritan New England. Consequently, they were heirs in a meaningful way to the region's habits of conscience and behavior, both private and public, in matters personal and those dealing with policy. Much of their work as judges reflects the Puritan ethic—secularized to be sure, but with roots in the minds of eighteenth-century New Englanders.

The Puritan ethic, which lay at the heart of the Taft-Holmes moral estate, is itself a complex but easily discernible set of principles. Taken together, the effect is one of an elitist mentality. A leading characteristic is distrust of power of whatever kind: Power corrupts because man is corruptible. Another fundamental insists on the dignity and equality of all people, as a creature of God or as a spark from a divine force. Such seemingly contrary tenets are resolved—to a degree, at least—by a confidence and an optimism, a deep-seated conviction that right will prevail over evil because God is good or Nature beneficent. In combination these principles advanced a highly moralistic code of belief and behavior, one to which Taft and Holmes, in their distinctive ways, sought to be true. Taft, the advocate of power distributed to branches and levels of government, held that the judiciary is the balance wheel of the constitutional system. Holmes, the skeptic, also at times was willing to restrain power, including that of the courts, in the name of a common good. Both men respected the rights of the individual, but always with boundaries established in law. More than Holmes, Taft may be viewed as "a man of good hope" sustained by the belief that somehow things would work out right. No doubt Holmes's Civil War experience played havoc with such an attitude. As he remarked later, after the Civil War things never seemed the same again. Within self-imposed limits, Holmes continued to judge case after case in a way that said respect for the law is the source of whatever hope the human race might have. On the 1920s court the optimistic Taft faced off against the realistic Holmes as they cooperated and competed in interpreting and applying the Constitution.

More particularly, what was the nature of the Puritan political legacy that these jurists were likely to draw on consciously, or at times unconsciously? Only in the eighteenth century did Puritan spokesmen begin fully to expound on man and government in ways exhibiting secular overtones. Commentators, mostly clergymen, from John Wise to Ezra Stiles, had in their writings come slowly but with certainty to embrace modes of secular political thinking. As applied to civil rule they helped shape the ideas of a revolutionary generation. The success of the movement for independence was assured by adoption of the Constitution. Prior approval of these great events by men of God meant two things: One, God was made to appear on the side of the American people; and, two, Puritan influences behind this divine approbation were carried into the nineteenth century and beyond. Taft and Holmes would accept Puritan thought as part of their political, and thus juridical, past—what had helped make them what they were and how they came to be. An understanding of this process requires reference to what these eighteenth-century divines had once advanced as sound political theory.

Among the earliest Puritan preachers to display an affinity for secular principles as applied to church government but applicable to civil government as well, was John Wise (1652–1725), minister of the congregation at Ipswich. By relying heavily on the work of Samuel von Pufendorf in *De Jure Naturae et Gentium*, Wise formulated a defense of congregationalism against the encroachments of presbyterian church organization; and he did so in a way that had a ready bearing on civil self-government. Among the principles Wise advanced were "self-love and self-preservation as being dominant in every man's being," that man's liberty was "instampt upon his rational nature," and an "equality amongst men." From there Wise went on to assert that "the formal reason of government is the will of the community. The chief end of civil communities is that men conjoined may be secured against the injuries they are liable to from their own kind." In short, he stated a remarkably advanced piece of political theory as the New England colonies were in the early stages of putting self-rule into practice.[14]

Elisha Williams (1694–1755), a Harvard graduate, had been rector at Yale from 1725 to 1739. Writing under the pen name "Philalethes," he put forth a treatise, "The Essential Rights and Liberties of Protestants," a document that expressed sympathy for the basic features of the commercial revolution. "Reason tells us all are born naturally equal, i.e., with equal right to their persons, so also, with an equal right to their preservation, and therefore such things as Nature affords for their subsistence." Whereupon Williams/Philalethes delivered a defense of the rights of property. In this respect, he wrote, in part:

> and every man having a property in his person, the labour of his body and the work of his hands are properly his own to which no one has a right but himself. . . . Thus every man has a natural right to (or being proprietor of) his own person and his own actions and labour and to what he can honestly acquire by his labor, which we call property. . . . And if every man has a right to his person and property he also has a right to defend them.

Such passages leave little doubt that in Puritan political tracts property was viewed as having a sacred character. Considering that such ideas mingled with arguments in favor of the rights of conscience, property rights were essential to the operation of the Protestant ethic, which received some of its most persuasive expression in the writings of New England churchmen.[15]

In offering a defense of the right of revolution, Jonathan Mayhew (1720–1766) marked a further maturation of Puritan-related political ideas. As a colonial American and clergyman, he urged the mother country to drive the French from North America. Mayhew's reasons were political: the French system of government was absolutist, as well as religious: as a people, the French were Catholic and therefore priest-ridden. Both of these facts gave him concern about the freedom of the individual under law. Mayhew argued that unless the French were forced to yield their claims, the Anglo-American advance across the continent faced containment. Clearly, he was concerned with worldly affairs, at the center of which were his views on the right of revolution. "A Discourse Concerning Unlimited Submission and Non-Resistance To The Higher Power," written in 1750, is a long, somewhat involved series of arguments, based, it appears at first, on the teachings of St. Paul. As Mayhew moved from point to point in his polemic it becomes clear that Paul is merely the occasion, Mayhew's notions becoming far more historical than scriptural. As he insisted at one juncture, "nothing can well be imagined more directly contrary to common sense than to suppose that millions of people could be subjected to the arbitrary, precarious pleasure of a single man." His appeal was to common sense rather than divine purpose. The power of such an arbitrary ruler, or a set of such men, pretended to have authority over person and property, and in itself that justified revolution. In virtual anticipation of the events of 1776, Mayhew wrote: "A people really oppressed to a great degree by their sovereign cannot be insensible when they are so oppressed. . . . For a nation thus abused to arise simultaneously, and to resist their prince, even to dethroning him, is not a criminal act, but a justifiable way of indicating their liberties and their rights." In fact, Mayhew had the history of Charles I in mind, but there is a prophetic ring in his call upon reason to justify history past and history future. Finally, the conclusion of this discourse sounded familiar notes and phrasing. "Let us all learn to be free and loyal. Let us not profess ourselves vassals to the lawless pleasure of any man on earth. But let us remember at the same time, government is sacred, and not to be trifled with." Within a quarter of a century of the publication of this Discourse, the reigning monarch of England took on some of the characteristics of Charles Stuart, thereby inviting revolution.[16]

As years went by, one after another Puritan sermon repeated such radical refrains. Abraham Williams (1727–1784), basing a sermon on I Cor. xii, 25, could conclude the voice of the people was the voice of God, and that though in society people must keep their place such a dictum was true for the governor and the governed alike.[17] In May 1775, Samuel Langdon (1725–1797), as president of Harvard, was invited to give the Election Day sermon at Watertown. This was within a month of Lexington and Concord. His text was Isaiah I:26, and there can be no doubt where his sentiments lay.

Every nation, when able and agreed, has a right to set up over themselves any form of government that to them may appear most conducive to the common welfare. The excellency of the constitution has been the boast of Great Britain, and the envy of neighboring nations. . . . But in what does the British nation's law glory? In titles of a mere shadow of its ancient political system. The pretense for taxing America has been that the nation contracted an immense debit for the defense of the American colonies. . . .

But can the amazing national debt be paid by a little trifling sum squeezed year to year out of America?

In Langdon, theories were giving way to reasons why the king and parliament might be defied, a highly combustible proposition.[18]

Closing out the century was Ezra Stiles (1727–1795). Stiles wrote *A History of Three of the Judges of King Charles I*, about men who had taken refuge in Connecticut. The book gave him an opportunity to descant on the rights of the people, sometimes in a singularly aggressive way. His praise of the Jacobin societies as having proved "the salvation of France" and his rejoicing at the execution of Louis XVI must have dismayed many of his readers. To him, "the very notion of petitioning parliaments, national councils, or kings for rights and liberties was a badge of slavery." Rights existed in nature and were not within the bounty of kings or any form of government to bestow. Insurrection against despots was deemed just because in that way the political order might be renovated. Stiles condemned Bastilles and Botany Bays with a fine impartiality, many of his passages taking on the character of a jeremiad.[19]

Looking at many of the observations of these New England divines, it is not difficult to identify similarities with the convictions of Taft and Holmes. John Wise's appeal to self-love and self-preservation might easily have come from Sumner as he lectured at Yale, while the emphasis on property rights by Elisha Williams could be mistaken for quotations from Taft's court opinions. It must be remembered, too, that Oliver Wendell Holmes was very much a capitalist, differing little from Taft in that respect. Appeals to reason were the eighteenth-century equivalent of the enshrining of science from the 1850s on. Insisting on common sense rather than divine purpose in viewing the relationship of people to government would hardly have garnered a dissent from either man. Certainly Ezra Stiles's approval of the Jacobin societies would have shocked Taft more than Holmes, but both would have agreed with Samuel Langdon's assertion that "every nation, when able and agreed, has a right to set up over themselves any form of government . . . conducive to the common welfare." These and like principles spinning out of clerical declamation are reminders of how religious minds generated political prescriptions common to the age of reason that were acceptable to Taft and Holmes well into the twentieth century.

With no particular reference to Taft or Holmes, but in a way certainly encompassing them, two astute foreign observers of the American experience have said as much. Andre Siegfried, the noted French student of America, contended that if you want to understand the real sources of national inspiration you must go back to the Puritans.[20] In his *The American Commonwealth*, James Bryce was more explicit when he identified "a hearty Puritanism" pervading the constitution as it came from the hands of the Founding Fathers.[21]

And what of the larger frame of reference, the New England of the nineteenth century, where and when a latter-day Puritan intellectualism might figure positively or negatively among the best minds of the period? There were competing sources of inspiration: transcendentalism, German idealism, English romanticism; but the old faith was an element that persisted. Some saw Emerson as a misguided Puritan; Hawthorne, no doubt, was obsessed with a Puritan sense of sin; Holmes's father, the Autocrat, referred to French realism in the novel as "swampy, malodorous, ill-smelling patches of soil which had been previously left to reptiles and vermin." What took place in New England in the early decades of the century was nothing less than an American renaissance which, though it might point to the future as in the writings of Herman Melville, was nonetheless grounded in the Puritan past. Its impact dissipated slowly. The poet, Edwin Arlington Robinson (Holmes's distant relative) remained a semi-Puritan in much of his work well into the twentieth century. As for Taft and Holmes, they were very much nineteenth-century New Englanders moved along by fast-flowing intellectual currents as they tried to deal with the tensions arising from the conflict of faith and science. The path from Puritanism to pragmatism was not always easy to negotiate. Though both men traveled it, they reacted differently along the way, which helps to account for their different visions of the law.

2
The Times and the Judges

THE CERTITUDES THAT DOMINATED THE AMERICAN MIND AT THE MID-point of the nineteenth century were impugned and in some instances shattered by new findings in the biological and physical sciences. The blow thus delivered to supernaturalism has been called "the most striking fact in [American] intellectual history of the last one-third of the century."[1] Yet the impact of Darwin's *Origin of Species* went well beyond the damage done to revealed religion. Constitutional government grounded on the Newtonian concept of balanced order—the work ethic that carried with it respect for the individual's place in the capitalistic economic system, law derived from certain a priori axioms, in sum, the very fabric of society—was to be rewoven from old materials into new patterns of thought and behavior. Just where William Howard Taft and Oliver Wendell Holmes would fit in the new scheme of things could hardly be predicted. But one thing is certain, they would think differently and judge differently than had their fathers before them.[2]

During the period between 1859, the year Darwin published his seminal work, and 1865, when Lee surrendered at Appomattox, the American nation had little inclination and less energy to engage itself with the social implications of Darwin's theses. America was engaged in a great civil war, testing whether the nation would endure or fragment: the defining moment in the history of the republic. Following hard on the heels of the war came what Richard Hofstadter has called "the vogue of Social Darwinism."[3] Far more so than in Darwin's England, the United States was to become a living laboratory for experimentation in the process of which scientific materialism was to be both presupposition and product. Poised to replace religion as the moral force in the country, science succeeded in doing so to a significant degree among the classes if not the masses.

There had been nonsupernatural ways of thinking in earlier generations. Rationalism, deism, free-thinking could be readily identified from earlier times, only to do battle with a Christian faith that rejected such philosophies as unacceptable to a God-fearing people. Furthermore, Darwinism had not given a sudden birth to the theory of evolution; it should be viewed, instead, as a continuation of a long line of evolutionary speculation, European certainly and in some sense American. For example, John Winthrop IV, Professor of Natural Philosophy at Harvard, writing in 1755, sought an explanation of earthquakes in science, sounding like an incipient evolutionary. He assigned natural causes to such phenomena rather than to the wrath of God as a secondary cause derived from a First Cause. To be sure, such teachings as Winthrop's touched very few people. Orthodoxy prevailed; still, Winthrop, among others, and Benjamin Franklin especially, was trying to grasp the natural mysteries by scientific means.[4]

Eighteen-seventy marked a decided change in the attitude of numerous religious leaders as these new currents swept through the realms of thought. There occurred on the part of believers an attempt to seek accommodation between supernaturalism and science. Asa Gray, Holmes's Harvard professor and a man he greatly admired, wrote to this effect as early as 1860. To Gray, a devout Christian, natural selection was not contradictory to, but consistent with, the divine design of the universe. John Fiske reached a much wider audience with *Outlines of Cosmic Philosophy*, published in 1874. Also a Harvard professor, Fiske asserted that evolution was indeed part of God's plan, that the Divine Mind revealed to man a greater complexity than had ever been laid bare before. With one and the same line of reasoning, the omniscience of God and the truths of science were of a single piece. Fiske's book went through many editions and did much to neutralize the seeming contradictions between church and laboratory. In *Evolution and Religion* (1885), Henry Ward Beecher, the most famous preacher of his day, declared quite simply that evolution was the "deciphering" of God's thought. His frank and open compromise gained Beecher a host of followers, in both pulpits and pews.[5]

Nonphilosophical explanations of change had been present in American life from the founding of the colonies. The existence of the frontier, to which generation after generation had repaired, gave the strong impression that in America nothing was fixed or final. Radical technological advances reaffirmed the feeling that a continuous process was at work in remaking the socioeconomy. A rigid system of inherited traditions and institutions typical of older societies was lacking. The form of the national government—a constitutional, federal union—was looked upon as an unfinished experiment. Such conditioning factors further prepared the ground for a scientific definition of mankind's origins and destiny.

Advocates of natural selection argued that life is a matter of struggle to survive, struggle that leads to change, and change that amounted to progress. Mutation, not fixity, was the watchword. The so-called laws governing the universe were subject to reinterpretation as science discovered new facts and reworked old ones. The laws of society were subject to a similar process: Change was not determined by what people chose to believe or do, but what they were required to believe, in light of ever enlarging scientific discoveries. As Charles Peirce was to remark: "that which I can not but believe is for me true." There was a mechanistic quality to this early version of science applied to society, which tended to reduce the species to the status of a product of forces beyond human control. Survival of the fittest, taken in isolation, replaced moral suasion with force as a social determinant. In the beginning, 'man was with animal and man was animal' could well have been the first verse of the gospel according to William Graham Sumner. This and other evolutionary postulates were grist from Sumner's mill as he lectured at Yale and spoke to audiences around the country—propositions William Howard Taft well remembered. Such teachings spread beyond the confines of academe. Andrew Carnegie, writing in 1889, put it this way: "Although the natural law of competition is sometimes hard on the individual, it is best for the race since it insures the survival of the fittest."[6] As Sumner asked: who could believe in the survival of the weakest, that would be the law of anti-civilization. In his essay, "The Absurd Effort to Make the World Over,"[7] he proposed to expose the fallacy of reform legislation, the laws of which Taft and Holmes, as judges, would have to deal with.

Although they retained elements of Social Darwinism in their outlook, neither Taft nor Holmes was to espouse the doctrine in its crudest form. The two men had come under various other influences, including traditional values, democratic impulses, republican principles, life experiences. And they lived in an age when mechanistic evolution was itself being transformed into a far more humanistic system, one that could be made consistent with established values—in short, a pragmatic system. The concept of man as an individual, worthy in self and capable of managing his own destiny, was not to succumb to the rule of force after all. Whether grounded in philosophy, ancient or modern, or in religion, supernatural or humanistic, this Western idea of man's intrinsic value could be adopted by the scientifically minded and traditionally minded alike. This was the magic appeal of the pragmatic method.

One of the distinguishing characteristics of Western history is the belief that mankind has the power to exert greater and greater control over physical nature. Pragmatism proposed to enhance that ability when applied to the social order. According to William James, Holmes's friend and associate in the late 1860s and early 1870s, old ideas were wedded to new ideas to produce new truth. Such a way of thinking was particularly apposite a legal system. The mind of man was free to make laws of behavior in all forms of human activity. Because all past laws were now recognized as adaptations, responses to past conditions, so new laws were to be fashioned to deal with new conditions. The greater the change of old to new, the greater the need to act quickly in order to make law relevant. There was nothing fixed or final in the law; therefore, nothing was absolutely right or absolutely wrong. Lacking any other standard for judging the worth of a law, pragmatism advanced the test of workability. A law that works for the individual or for society is valid because it is useful. Pragmatism was an instrument seeking an outlet in action, not a system of thought; nevertheless, pragmatism did provide a way out of the blind alley where an unmodified determinism necessarily led. Holmes embraced the pragmatic reading of law fully, and Taft, despite misgivings, could hardly ignore it.

Even so, the critical issue spawned by pragmatism went unanswered. Nor did the pragmatist as purist attempt to give an answer. The question remained: What set of values would be brought to bear to verify workability? Workability according to whom? Conservatives might agree that if legislation was to be utilized to eliminate the worst abuses of capitalism, such laws would be wholesome and, more to the point, constitutional. More likely, however, liberals—whether populist or progressive, labor leader or social worker, preacher of the social gospel or socialist with a new creed—would insist on the use of new and untried legal measures to promote a great variety of reforms. Both Taft and Holmes, the former as President and the latter when on the Supreme Court, came to support reform. Their motivation was different, based both on their vision of the character and function of the law and on its desired effects; but agree, they did. The law did have its uses. Taft's war on trusts and Holmes's commitment to the rule of law in the historic 1911 anti-trust cases represent a convergence of presidential and judicial uses of the Sherman Act as the nation sought to impose limits on corporate power.

Such events were far in the future as young Taft entered Ohio politics, first as an assistant district attorney for Hamilton county, then as collector of internal revenue for the first Ohio district, and in 1887, seven years out of law school, appointed to the Superior Court of Ohio (he was elected to a full term the next year). For his part, Holmes immersed himself in the intellectual pursuits of the Metaphysical Club, an informal gathering of junior savants in and around Cambridge as they cast up answers, almost as one casts dice, to penetrate the riddle of man and the cosmos. Soon, Holmes was practicing law, revising Kent's *Commentaries* for a twelfth edition, and lecturing on the constitution at the Law School—all this before publication of his great book, *The Common Law.* A year later, in 1882, he was named to the Supreme Judicial Court of Massachusetts. For the next fifty years, in Boston and then in Washington, Holmes sat in judgment on the law: its meaning, its purpose, its uses and abuses. It is the two early judgeships, Taft in Ohio and Holmes in Massachusetts, that hold the first case law indications of the distinctive jurisprudence each was to become known by.

When Taft was serving on the Superior Court of Ohio and the Sixth Federal Circuit the issue of property rights was central to his decision-making as the cases came before him. So central in fact was property (unavoidably so in his appellate capacity), it became the organizing principle in his early judicial career. To better appreciate the function of property in Taft's jurisprudence it is useful to look more closely at the teachings of William Graham Sumner, his well-remembered university professor. During the 1870s—the years he was an undergraduate at Yale—Taft's foremost teacher was even then refining his convictions about property and the social order, ideas he was to expand on and publish in the years to come. As he was later to write: "The most limiting condition in the status of human societies is the ratio of the number of their members to the amount of land at their disposal." This Sumner called "the man-land ratio." One corollary of this proposition arising from the importance of land was a deep and perennial reverence for property, seen as the sophisticated version of land in advanced civilizations. Thus, for Sumner, property rights became "the most universal interest of mankind."[8] As such they must be guarded at all cost because progressive civilizations depended on sanctity of private property.

Unlike Sumner, Taft did not agree that property rights by definition exceeded in value the natural rights of man as based on reason; nonetheless, an examination of his court decisions shows that his understanding of natural rights was intimately connected to the possession and protection of property in whatever form, including, of course, corporate wealth. As an examination of two important extra-court writings demonstrates, Taft would wrestle with the often conflicting demands of property and natural human rights. In an essay appearing in the *Michigan Law Journal* for August 1894, and in an address before the American Bar Association the next year, Taft faced squarely the quandary of which competing rights to favor.[9] What emerges from his writings, as well as his Court opinions, is a strong inclination to protect property rights as the bedrock of superior civilizations while at the same time leaving room for the further development of the rights of labor in a capitalist socioeconomy. Apparently the legal problems involved continued to occupy his mind when serving as secretary of war in Roosevelt's cabinet. In 1908, Taft addressed the Cooper Union Institute in New York City, choosing as the theme of his remarks "Labor and Capital."[10] This latter speech is better analyzed in a later chapter, showing, as it does, Taft's maturing outlook on the issues. It is cited here to emphasize the ongoing concerns Judge Taft had for property rights in a free society. Indeed it is preferable to study his court opinions—both as a state and a federal judge, as well as his work as solicitor general—before taking up his 1894 and 1895 writings in detail.

In their judgeships both Taft and Holmes faced changing times as the America of the 1880s and 1890s revealed growing discontent within the ranks of society's have-nots, and a disillusionment with the Constitution and the judges who interpreted it to the advantage of the rich and powerful. The Populist movement, which drew its strength from the Plains states but appealed to pockets of agrarian discontent wherever located, threatened to redefine American politics through the emergence of a viable third party. Mary K. Lease urged the farmers of Kansas to raise more hell and less corn, and Ignatius Donnelly of Minnesota spoke the message of *j'accuse*: "corruption dominates the ballot box, the legislatures, the Congress and touches even the ermine of the bench."[11] Impressive Congressional victories accompanied Colonel James B. Weaver's challenge to the two-party system when, in the presidential election of 1892, he won more than a million popular votes. At least twelve Congressmen called themselves Populists when the fifty-second Congress convened.

By capturing the spirit of discontent and aspiration within the organization of the Democratic party William Jennings Bryan became the embodiment of the farmers' hopes for the future. To the Republicans and to men of property whatever their political affiliation, Bryan was a prophet of doom as he did battle against what he deemed the forces of evil. Though not thoughtlessly opposed to change, both Taft and Holmes grew apprehensive at these developments in national politics, especially when they discerned a threat to the reign of law and order. And slurs made on the integrity of the judiciary they might take personally, making them all the more suspicious of the good intentions of the agrarian reformers.

Across the nation, farmer discontent was accompanied and then outstripped by industrial disturbances, which appeared to men of the judges' persuasion to be the more dangerous because the disturbances led to menacing confrontations between the factory proletariat and the capitalist owners. There was an undeniable odor of class struggle in the great strikes of the period: International Harvester in 1886, Homestead and Coeur d'Alene in 1892, and Pullman in 1894. The pattern in these and other disputes was much the same: When labor organized and resorted to strikes and boycotts in its efforts to improve hours, wages, and working conditions the full force of the law was felt, as represented by injunctions against workers and the use of troops. Scabs were imported, strikes were broken, and union leaders went to jail.

The ugly mood this trend of events produced was impossible to disguise. The law was unmistakably on the side of privilege and property. Judges—Taft more so than Holmes—were seen by labor as the minions of the plutocracy. Close examination of Taft's record tends to indicate that such a judgment was simplistic. But, understandably, as he was disinclined to break openly with his judicial brethren, the fine legal distinctions that inhered in certain of his court opinions were lost on men who sat in jail cells for championing what they believed were the rights of the working class.

If the final decades of the nineteenth century were replete with industrial troubles because labor was determined to carry on the struggle with entrenched capitalism, Cincinnati was no more immune to disputes than other cities. Taft's most important decision when serving on the Ohio Superior Court grew out of a typical industrial stand-off. The case was *Moores & Company* v. *Bricklayers Union No. 1, W. H. Stephenenson, P. H. McElroy et al.* (1890).[12] The bricklayers became embroiled in a disagreement with a local builder, Parker Brothers. Unable to obtain satisfaction of their grievances, the union attempted to prevent materials from being sold to Parker Brothers by threatening to refuse supplies which other firms brought on Parker Brothers' job sites. Moores & Company, suppliers of limestone, was boycotted when it sought to deliver its wares to the building areas. A court of first instance awarded Moores damages, the case coming to the Superior Court on a motion for a new trial.

Taft's opinion upholding the lower court ruling was both erudite and favorable to property rights. He began by appealing to English common law, noting that "every man, be he capitalist, merchant, lawyer, or professional man is entitled to invest his capital, to carry on his business, to bestow his labor, or to exercise his calling, if within the law, according to his pleasure." In the case at hand, however, Taft held that under common law, "There are losses willfully caused to one by another in the exercise of what otherwise would be a lawful right, from simple motives of malice." He ruled that malice was the motivation of the bricklayers in their threats against Moores & Company, and he attempted to support this assertion by citing precedents from English law, remote in time and place from the matter before the court. While labor might combine as suitably as capital for reasons of self-advancement, worker organizations could not act on that account when the result was to interfere with property rights. Because property rights were, in theory, sacred, and nearly absolute before the law, the abstract rights of labor were denied in practice.

Not only had Taft embraced a double standard of social morality, to the detriment of labor, he had discovered "intent" and "malice" in the behavior of the bricklayers. Such a position ran counter to the assertions of the legal realist, of whom Holmes was becoming a leading advocate. Holmes was not interested in intention but in empirical results arising from the actions in question. He would have more likely asked, Were the effects of such actions good or bad, useful or not? Taft had gone fishing in the distant waters of history long past, an affront to the new jurisprudence, which was to prefer to take each case as it came to the court, and to judge it by an external standard of effects rather than by intention, real or supposed.

Taft remained an absolutist in his legal thinking. He may have been acquainted with the new scientific ways of thinking while at Yale, but his study of law at the Cincinnati Law School had proceeded along conservative lines. The ruling in the Moores case placed him with the overwhelming majority of his fellow judges of the time. He had not ruled on whim or fancy or malice of his own. Neither was he indifferent to the rights of the individual when they came in conflict with property rights, which certain of his later appeals court opinions will bear out. A further look into his Superior Court opinions anticipates this. In one case a man in a drunken stupor fell from a train and was killed. Taft ruled that his estate was entitled to compensation inasmuch as the train was not properly equipped to maintain passenger safety. In contrast, in another case he ruled to deny damages for a fourteen-year-old who, playing in a factory, accidentally lost a leg. Legally the factory owner was not liable in a matter of trespass. Clearly, Taft vacillated on the issue of property versus human rights; but just as clearly, he more often put property rights first.

Taft's appointment as Solicitor General of the United States comes close to being a quantum leap. After all, when named to the post, he had somewhat less than three years' experience as a state jurist, judging state law. Perhaps it is anachronistic to say that the Solicitor General was looked upon as the "tenth justice," the office having been created only in 1870, the year Congress set up the Department of Justice. In so doing, the law stipulated that the appointee "shall be . . . an officer learned in the law, to assist the Attorney General in the performance of his duties, to be called Solicitor General."[13] When Taft held the post it was still in its early growth stage. Many years later, while serving as Chief Justice, he acted to give to the Solicitor General great influence in determining which cases deserved to be argued before the high court, one of the provisions of the Judges Act of 1925 being the writ of certiorari. Such was not the case later in the nineteenth century, when all cases appealed to the Supreme Court were heard, whether they were significant in law or otherwise.

As it happened, Taft's appointment as Solicitor General rested largely on political grounds, and not because of his mastery of constitutional law. Ohio's governor, Joseph P. Foraker, a political power broker almost without peer, suggested that Taft be named to the Supreme Court when another Cincinnati man of the law turned down the offer. President Harrison, aware of Taft's limited judicial experience, agreed to name him Solicitor General, which in itself may be an indication that the office had not yet attained much stature. Because "learned in the law" was one of the statutory requirements of the post, it meant that the new appointee had to deepen *and* broaden his knowledge of the constitution and the laws passed pursuant to it. This, Taft gladly did.

The most notable success the young barrister achieved had to do with the *Bering Sea* case (1891).[14] At issue was the taking of seals by British fishermen from the Bering Sea, over which the United States claimed jurisdiction as part of the Alaska Purchase Treaty of 1867. London instituted a case before the Supreme Court, seeking to enjoin the executive branch of the federal government from taking measures appropriate to the protection of American interests. Taft argued the case for the United States on the principle that, inasmuch as America and Britain were at the time engaged in negotiations over fishing rights in the Bering Sea, a foreign power could not pursue litigation aimed at causing the Court to censure the conduct of another branch of the national government. The Supreme Court concurred. In another case won by Taft, the issue involved the legality of the collection of customs under the McKinley Tariff of 1890. The point of dispute was whether the law had been constitutionally passed, since Speaker of the House Reed had counted numerous representatives present even though they took no part in the voting. The Court ruled that such members could be legally included, thereby making up the necessary quorum. Such bright spots were not common in the work of the Solicitor General, however. What needs to be stressed, therefore, is the period of two years during which Taft became more and more knowledgeable about federal law, essential to his appointment to the Sixth Federal Appeals Court, and just possibly an added consideration should he ever be seriously considered for the Supreme Court.

In March 1892, Congress acted to provide an additional judge for each United States Circuit Court: Taft was the obvious nominee for the Sixth Circuit (Cincinnati). He took his seat that year, remaining in the office for the next eight years. During this period Taft continued to use property rights as the benchmark against which other claims on government must be weighed. At the same time, he displayed a growing awareness that the rights of property might well have to be balanced against the interest of the community, especially the rights of labor. The first important case in which Judge Taft had a hand was *Toledo, Ann Arbor and Northern Michigan Railway Company v. Brotherhood of Locomotive Engineers* (1893).[15] The railway had instituted a case in equity, seeking an injunction in federal district court against the locomotive engineers who had struck the company. In an effort to isolate the railroad, the workers threatened not to handle any freight on lines connecting with the Toledo, Ann Arbor and Northern Michigan system. On appeal, Taft upheld the injunction issued by the lower court, finding that interstate commerce had been unduly disturbed.

Taking much of his reasoned argument from his state opinion in the Moores & Company case, Taft conceded that a man had an "inalienable right to bestow his labor as he will, and to withhold his labor where he will." Exceptions arose when organized workers made use of the secondary boycott, thereby interfering with the property of other companies not party to the original dispute. Also in the action of the engineers, Taft found elements of intentional malice. His conservative jurisprudence prompted him to read intent into the actions of the defendants, while blinding him to possible malice on the part of the railroad owners. His entire position had a definite Sumnerian quality to it: property rights as the foundation stone of the economic system could not be weakened. During his tenure as Appeals Court judge, Taft was to issue a number of anti-labor injunctions, and he soon developed the reputation of being anti-union.

In 1894, Taft sentenced Frank Phelan—an aide to Eugene V. Debs, president of the American Railway Union—to six months in jail for contempt of court. The incident was an outgrowth of the great Pullman strike of that year. Debs's union had come to the assistance of strikers at the Pullman Palace Car Company by ordering members of the American Railway Union to refuse to handle trains of which Pullman cars were a part. Phelan had been assigned by Debs to the Cincinnati area, to tie up rail traffic there. He was arrested for obstructing the business of the New Orleans & Texas Pacific Railway, at the time in federal receiver-ship. Taft cited Phelan when informed that he had refused to obey an injunction against union action. The ruling rested on the legal consid-eration that the company in question was in federal bankruptcy proceed-ings and thus was protected by the law. Given these circumstances, Taft believed he had no choice but to proceed in this way, though it was the sort of legalism labor rejected as a ruse.

On the face of it, In re: Phelan[16] was another effort to protect property rights whatever the cost. What makes the case remarkable is that, in the course of his opinion, Taft articulated a clear judicial definition and defense of the right to strike. He conceded that employees were justified in organizing a union for the purpose of taking action respecting the full range of their grievances. This benefited the workers and the public at large. As Taft put it: "workers have labor to sell." By standing together they were in a better position to command higher prices for their labor than would have been possible were they to act singly against a powerful employer. Unions, furthermore, were in perfect keeping with the law and the common sense of the matter in accumulating funds which might be helpful in winning disputes with owners. The whole apparatus of labor organization found favor with Taft, including union leadership for rank-and-file workers, strike votes, and union discipline. All these elements must be present, thought Taft, if labor was to be able to satisfy its demands in an industrial society.

For his time and judicial position, Judge Taft was unusually supportive of labor. It was logical, therefore, that he wanted to explain exactly the grounds on which he had proceeded in the Phelan case. If Phelan had come to Cincinnati to urge a peaceful strike and it had been successful, the railway company would have had no complaint at law and Phelan would not have been cited for contempt. He could have called the strike because of unsatisfactory terms of employment and would have been within the law. But, in fact, Phelan's purpose was to exercise the force of a secondary boycott against the Pullman Company. Such a boycott was simply illegal. In the concluding passages of his opinion Taft explained the issue in its fullest meaning. "If the orders of the court are not obeyed, the next step is anarchy." Frank Phelan was sent to jail, Taft referring to the sentence as "a most disagreeable duty."[17] He did not want to punish Phelan severely, but he was equally reluctant to be easy on him, reasoning that that would encourage others to break the law.

Much of the significance of Taft's opinion in the Phelan case sprang from the fact that he had brought organized labor, at least in his court, out of the legal shadows. While he continued to differentiate between a strike and a boycott that adversely affected third parties, he had nonetheless laid out a strongly reasoned justification for the existence of organized labor and of its rights. In so doing, Taft had exhibited a sense of juridical independence. By 1894, the judge had seen enough of life and the law to cause him to attenuate, perhaps essentially, the dogmatic assertions of Professor Sumner which rejected any concept of rights not resting on superior strength.

Two further cases demonstrated Taft's sense of fair play for workers. In the *Voight Case* (1896), he ruled that an employer, in this instance a railroad company, was liable for injuries suffered by a workman while he was on the job, thereby rejecting the old common law principle of assumed risk on the part of the worker.[18] At the same time he weakened, to a degree, the sanctity of contract rule, inasmuch as the employee in question had signed an agreement relieving the company of liability for injuries that might be incurred on the job. Admittedly, the Supreme Court was to reverse Taft's ruling; but vindication had to wait several years, until passage of the federal Employers Liability Act in 1908, and its subsequent acceptance by the Supreme Court. Taft had flown his reform colors some time in advance of the Progressive Movement, though there was as much a sense of fair play in the Voight opinion as there was a commitment to the still unformed ways of Progressivism. Not so in the other two appeals court judgments he handed down.

Similarly, in the *Narramore Case* (1899) the Cleveland, Chicago and St. Louis Railway Company was liable for injury to a brakeman, due to safety violations by the company of which the worker was aware and had accepted as part of his job.[19] Taft presented a cogent argument in deciding the case against the railroad. The substance of his position was that a law had been enacted stipulating safety work rules on railroads operating in the state of Ohio. The purpose of the legislative act had been to protect the worker by statute because there was no other means of affording minimum safety conditions. Liberty of contract, further- more, did not allow an employee "to contract himself out of the statute." He must be covered by the safety code, willingly or unwillingly. Taft also stated that the payment of a fine by the company to the state, and not damages to the victim, would make such a regulation "not much more than a dead letter." On the contrary, the purpose of the legislation was clear: to protect railroad employees from evident sources of danger. It would serve both labor and the public ill if employees were able "to waive compliance." "This court," Taft concluded, "will not recognize nor enforce such an agreement." In rendering this judgment he was striking out on his own, wherever that might lead.

Taft was also, on occasion, prepared to move against the corporation itself. At least one important case, that involving the Addystone Pipe and Steel Company in 1898, caused him to invoke the Sherman Anti- trust Act.[20] He found that the company had conspired with other manu- facturers of cast-iron pipe to fix prices and thus reduce competition. The facts of the case were surprisingly similar to those in the much publicized *E. C. Knight Case* (1895), in which the Supreme Court had resoundingly rejected application of the Sherman law to alleged price fixing in sugar. The Knight ruling was widely seen as upholding the absolute nature of property rights because the American Sugar Refining Company, the defendant in the case, controlled ninety-five percent of the sugar refining capacity in the country. Yet the Court decided it was not in violation of the contract, combination, and conspiracy provisions of the 1890 law. Taft dared to take a different line, insisting that, in the case before him, the sales contracts that actually fixed prices constituted restraint of trade between the states. More surprising still, before 1901, the Supreme Court, in a rare application of the Sherman Act, affirmed Taft's judgment.

During the period of his early judgeships William Howard Taft was, for the most part, a case and court jurist. Only infrequently did he choose to range beyond the work of the day, to stand back from the law as it operated in fact in order to ponder larger propositions of law, not so much as an abstraction but of its force and meaning in society. At midpoint in the years he was preoccupied with hearing cases argued and rendering his decisions, he did, however, take the occasion to set down certain principles as essential to his jurisprudence. The first of these, "The Right of Private Property," took the form of an address to the graduating class at the Law School of the University of Michigan. It was published in the August 1894 issue of the *Michigan Law Journal*. It is in fact a basic document in the Taft canon, learned and measured, conservative yet cognizant of the need for ordered change.

A year later, before a meeting of the American Bar Association, Taft delivered his "Recent Criticism of the Federal Judiciary." In this address, which was more practical in its orientation, Taft nevertheless found it appropriate to reiterate certain principles of his legal philosophy, which makes it a companion piece to the Law School address. The timing of these excursions into the realms of history and contemporary society and the nature and place of law in a future fraught with change is significant. Freed of the constraint to express his ideas in response to the points of law in a given suit, Taft was able to explain himself and his commitment to government under law more fully and more effectively than at any time before.

"The Right to Private Property" proves to be Taft's major statement, concerned as it is with the most pivotal proposition in the whole of his juridical creed.[21] But it is much more than that: It comes down to a testament to the centrality of private property in the whole scheme of Western civilized society. Written with an unmistakable gravity of purpose, directed as it was to a new generation of lawyers, the statement unabashedly champions the "economic man"—and this at a juncture in Western history when capitalism faced increasing criticism, even some self-doubts. Making an initial appeal to history long passed, Taft said: "As far back as we can go in the history of the common law in England, the right of property of the freeman was theoretically inviolate." He then quoted from the Magna Carta to this effect. Well aware that such guarantees have been ignored in history, nonetheless, "the ancient charter and the pledge of rights became more sacred." Consequently, with the founding of the English colonies in North America, with the development of colonies into states at the time of independence, with independence itself and in the new federal constitution, Taft found in the language of all the pertinent documents the pervasive influence of the Magna Carta. Quoting from the North West Ordinance, he noted the following provision: "No man shall be deprived of his liberty or property but by the judgment of his peers or the law of the land . . . and no law ought ever to be made to . . . interfere with or effect private contracts." The joining together in equal importance of personal liberty and the right of property was justified not only by the history of England but by that of his own country. Again the Bill of Rights was cited, referring to the Fifth Amendment, with Taft going on to argue that "the supreme court of the United States has held that the words 'due process' are the equivalent of the words of the Magna Carta." The due process clause of the Fourteenth Amendment is therefore merely a matter of consistently expanding the most worthwhile of objectives, a statement fully supported by the Supreme Court—that is, the "sacred" character of the right to private property.

It is at this early stage of his lengthy address that Taft states his most profound conviction regarding the American historical experience—namely, that "security of property and contract and liberty of the individual are indissolubly linked as the main props of higher and progressive civilization." Thus it became necessary on his part to be adamant about this linkage in light of radical theories of the state which were demanding that the right of private property be subordinated in the name of a new social order. What follows at this point is a statement of Taft's understanding of the philosophical underpinnings of the state. Exhibiting a mixture of influences, including the brutish views of Thomas Hobbes, the social contract of John Locke and the man-land ratio of William Graham Sumner, he contends that social justice requires that all men, laborers no less than the captain of industry, should be secure in enjoying the product of their work. The worker is free to withhold his labor, as is the capitalist to use his resources as he chooses. In Taft's view, the accumulation of capital has made the difference between barbarism and an advancing society. "Without it the whole world would still be groping in the darkness of the tribe." Whereupon Taft spelled out his socioeconomic code:

> Capital increases the amount of production and reduces the cost in labor units of each unit of production. The cheaper the cost of production the less each one had to work to earn the absolute necessities of life and the more time he had to earn its comforts. As material comforts increase the more

possible becomes happiness and the greater the opportunity for the cultivation of the higher instincts of the human mind and soul.

All this appears to have a certain textbook quality about it, redolent
perhaps of what Taft remembered from the time when Yale was given
over to Sumnerology.

The judge in Taft was especially anxious to demonstrate the interde-
pendence of labor and capital. In this regard his words continue to
exhibit a tendency to theorizing, at the same time prescinding from the
brutal realities of worker versus owner that were a feature of the 1880s
and 1890s in the United States: "Everything that tends legitimately to
increase the accumulation of wealth and its use for production will give
each laborer a larger share of the joint result of capital and his labor."
Taft openly disputed the charge of critics "of our present civilization"
that "the poor were getting poorer as the rich became richer, from which
premise it is said to follow that the wealth of the rich is unjustly
wrenched from the poor." At which point he added a touch of Malthus:
"Doubtless there is much misery in the world but there has always been."
Even this had a bright side, because the society of his time was more
aware of the depressed conditions under which so many lived, there had
occurred a greater spirit of "charity and benevolence" than had obtained
in ages past.

Taft nevertheless tended to worry about the accretion of wealth by
some individuals that was common to the age. He was sure that "men of
vision" deserved the enormous profits reaped by industry, but remained
dubious about wealth for the sake of wealth. To be socially acceptable,
profits should be plowed back into new industry, thereby providing an
ever-expanding market for labor. For Taft this was the proper scheme of
things. Self-interest was the driving force for all human activity, something especially obvious when it came to earning a living or making a
profit. It was the force that drove society forward, not backward.

At this juncture Taft's rationale for the right to private property
showed him in a new light. He lamented the corruption of legislatures
(no mention was made here of courts) by unscrupulous businessmen,
the managers of corporate wealth. Taft conceded that even personally
honest men could be dishonest in their business dealings because they
believed a different ethical code applied. Monopolies were yet another
source of mischief; he acknowledged "a righteous resentment among the
people" against the abuses arising from monopolies. In other words, men
of integrity were needed in the world of commerce and industry, but

labor leaders of wisdom and restraint were in equal demand. Taft went on to identify the Brotherhood of Locomotive Engineers as a model union in part because it avoided violence and intimidation. The radical labor leader was a threat to the principles of private property. Taft also expressed reservations about the entry of the labor movement into politics, apparently without admitting the paradox of big business dominant in his own Republican party. Still, he was hopeful labor leaders would "become educated by hard economic experience to the truth that they had a deep interest in maintaining the security of property rights." "All lovers of our country will say God speed the day."

In the final passages of his address Judge Taft returned to what, we must conclude, is the main theme of his words to the new lawyers. How can we stay the movement aimed at destroying property rights, he asked.

> By telling the truth and enforcing the truth that every laborer and every man of moderate means has as much interest to preserve the inviolability of corporate property as he has that of his own. . . . The friends and believers in our modern civilization with its security for private property, as the best means of the elevation of the race, must make their views and voices heard above the resounding din of anarchy, socialism, populism, and the general demagogy which is so wide spread today.

Taft concludes that the immediate burden of defending private property must fall upon the courts and those men of the law who bring cases before the judges.

That the federal courts were coming under heavy pressure from various quarters of public life was a growing challenge to the judges who administered the law. For example, of the first thirteen cases appealed to the Supreme Court, based on the Interstate Commerce Act of 1887, only one found a railroad guilty of transgressing the law. The Sherman Act did not fare much better with the federal judiciary, convinced as it was of the sacredness of private property. Indignation over "government by injunction" was the special grievance of the laboring class. Thus it was logical that William Howard Taft, who thought of the corps of federal judges as being virtually without fault, took the opportunity to defend the system against the charges leveled by its critics. In his 1895 address to the American Bar Association, "Recent Criticism of the Federal Judiciary," he minced no words, coming immediately to his main point.[22] "The principal charge against the Federal Courts is that they have flagrantly usurped jurisdiction, first, to protect corporations and perpetuate their many abuses, and, second, to oppress and destroy the

power of organized labor." Admitting that disaffection with the work of
the court was widespread, Taft set out to show that there was a general
misunderstanding of court procedures from which could be shown "the
causes why the judges could not exercise control, and it is necessarily
due to the character of the jurisdiction with which they are vested and
not to injustice in its exercise." His line of reasoning was singleminded
without being monolithic.

Judge Taft felt impelled to commence his defense by reference to the
federal union as it was constituted in 1787, along with mention of the
Kentucky Resolution (Virginia's role went unnoticed) in response to the
Alien and Sedition Acts, Marshall's decision in *Cohens* v. *Virginia*
(1821), and the Dred Scott case (1857). In each instance great public
controversy and hostility were aimed at the Court. Therefore one must
not be put off by controversy regarding the Court's position on the issues
of the 1880s and 1890s. Turning to those times, Taft laid down one of
his main premises: "The aim of all material civilization in its hard contest
with nature was the reduction of the costs of production." This struggle
was the main feature of the American experience in the post-Civil War
decades as the great corporations exploited the natural resources of the
nation and thereby accumulated great wealth, what Taft liked to call
"the rush to wealth." In the wake of this rush was corruption, due more
to corporate managers than to corporate owners (certainly an interesting
distinction). Many people came to view the corporation as the enemy;
this was especially true when any industry had been monopolized by one
corporate device—the trust. Such evils aside, however, and Taft honestly believed that they must not be allowed to persist, the corporation
was unique in bringing about progress and prosperity. Business had succeeded in its quest because private property rights had always been maintained. The Fourteenth Amendment had made it a federal responsibility
to protect the corporation against confiscation by either state regulator
or taxation. The size and scope of corporation activity, invariably interstate in character, required federal protection from local (i.e., state)
prejudice in matters of law and court rulings. Federal judges were sure
to be more objective than those of the states, and for this reason corporations sought relief from federal courts in defense of their business practices. "Corporate corruption can not be directly punished in the
Federal courts,"

> because the bribery of which many corporations are guilty is most difficult
> of legal proof, and crimes of this character are usually committed against the

State, so that Federal courts have no cognizance of them. It has been wisely settled by the adjudication of all courts, State and Federal, that the evils resulting from vesting in courts the power to set aside otherwise lawful acts of the legislature for alleged corruption in their passage, would exceed even the wrong done by such legislation because of the uncertainty it would give to the binding effect of all laws.

For Taft, "the main public evil of corporate wealth, the corruption of politics, must be reformed by the people and not by the courts." In this respect he was more inclined to fault the classes than the masses, because the intelligent, educated class had become so immersed in the "rush to wealth" that it spurned politics as a civic responsibility.

Taft then took up the contention that the Fourteenth Amendment, in using the word *person*, meant, or should have meant, only the recently freed slaves. But, he countered, if the corporation is not a person, surely the people who own the corporation are persons, and their property must be held inviolate. Further, and here he cited the *Knight* case, manufacturing or refining is not an act of transport or trade, and therefore it is not unlawful by the definitions stated in the Sherman Antitrust Act. Again admitting to the public's deep, popular distrust of the courts, Taft believed that, as the courts are by design conservators, as in railroad bankruptcy cases, they therefore seek to keep loss of capital at a minimum, as should be expected of conservators. He resorted to English case law and United States case law to support his position. In fact, Taft spent a good deal of attention on the execution of bankruptcy proceedings, setting out to prove what he assumed to be true.

Finally, Judge Taft took up the issue of "government by injunction," that is, the courts' hostility toward organized labor. His fundamental position—the more capital is able to act free of restraints, the more jobs there would be for labor—underlines his thinking. In so arguing he fell back on such phrases as "the law of supply and demand," "the natural law of struggle," and "the slow operation of natural laws." Labor must indeed organize for its own advancement; but, as with the courts, it must respect the right of private property. The problems labor experienced were not a matter of principle but of violence, fear, and intimidation in its methods. The courts must be alert to abuses on the part of both capital and labor. It may appear otherwise inasmuch as corporate corruption is done clandestinely, whereas labor boycotts are out in the open for all to see. Corporate actions are below the surface and difficult to prove, in contrast to the high profile of, say, the Pullman Strike of

1894, to which Taft made direct reference. When President Cleveland ordered his Attorney General, Richard Olney, to seek a court order enjoining workers from interfering with interstate rail operations as well as disrupting the United States mail, many public officials, including the governor of Illinois, were aghast. In attempting to justify government by injunction, Taft appeared uneasy, admitting that any number of right-thinking people looked upon the injunction as "an unwise stretching of a remedy in equity to meet an emergency which should have been met in other ways." He further conceded that the action taken only enhanced the view that the courts and the corporations were in collusion. Having said that, Taft foresaw anarchy if the law was not enforced, because the principle here was that right of private property, the alpha and the omega of the future Chief Justice's socioeconomic code.

Published in 1881, *The Common Law* is sometimes understood as Oliver Wendell Holmes's coming of age as a scholar.[23] Because Holmes was determined to do something of significance by the time he was forty, the appearance of this great book was perfectly timed. Yet, to appreciate how he prepared himself for his major accomplishment, attention needs to be given to earlier activities. The first such activity was his membership in the Metaphysical Club. Looking back, we can see that the club clearly boasted a remarkable collection of great minds: William James, Charles Peirce, Nicholas St. John Green, Chauncey Wright, Joseph Warren, John Chipman Grey along with Holmes. Each member was prepared to follow the paths of science in pursuit of his own ambition. Holmes himself "sensed" without at first knowing just how the law could be interpreted scientifically. During the years 1869–1873 he gradually came to understand how law and the scientific method could be merged. As he wrote to William James in April 1868: "The law as well as other series of facts in the world may be approached in the interests of science."[24] With time and reflection growing out of the spirited discussions that were a feature of the meetings of the Metaphysical Club, a scientific conception of the law became central to Holmes's efforts as a legal scholar and, in due season, as a sitting judge. He took his cue from Charles Peirce. Paraphrasing Peirce's admittedly awkward but widely accepted definition of pragmatic truth, Holmes was moved to ask us to consider what effects, that might conceivably have practical bearing, we conceive the law to have on society; then the effects of that law are the sum total of its validity, rendering it good or bad. Having arrived at the conviction that this scientific insight into the nature of man-made law was true and always had been so, Holmes took the crucial step leading him to his externalization thesis, wherein the law is judged by its results rather than by an abstract rule or principle. Up to this point in his thinking, however, the externalization rule was itself only a theory awaiting proof.

The chance opportunity to edit a new edition of Kent's *Commentaries* was also perfectly timed, with the twelfth edition appearing in 1873. The work involved in the editing assignment was no mere legal exercise. Holmes cited every relevant case and statute handed down or voted into law since the previous edition and took advantage of that to interpolate his ever-widening anthropological and historical learning. He endeavored to show the law as a response to the environment—political, social, or economic—and that, as conditions changed, so the law continued to respond in order to remain relevant. Holmes's efforts show the influence of John Stuart Mill and Fitzjames Stephen as the empirical elements became more pronounced in his understanding of the law, then and the law now. If law was to be evaluated properly, it must be according to empirical criteria, however much that might offend morality or sentiment. Work on the *Commentaries*—along with helping edit the *American Law Review*, which carried five of his essays—earned him an invitation to deliver the Lowell Lectures for 1880.

Refined and expanded, these lectures became *The Common Law*. In the opening sentence, Holmes speaks of his purpose: "to present a general view of the Common Law." He proposes a method: "We must alternately consult history and existing theories of legislation." And he states his objective: to understand the Law, for which "there are a great many rules which are quite sufficiently accounted for by their manifest good sense . . . [and] there are some which can only be understood by reference to the infancy of procedure among the German tribes, or to the social condition of Rome under the Decemvirs."[25]

Holmes first construed the early forms of liability, pointing out:

> customs, beliefs or needs of a primitive time establish a rule or formula. In the course of centuries the custom, belief or necessity disappears, but the rules remain. The reason which gave rise to the rule has been forgotten, and ingenious minds set themselves to inquire how it is to be accounted for. Some ground of policy is thought of which seems to explain it and reconcile it with the present state of things; and then the rule adapts itself to the new reasons which have been found for it, and enters a new career.

Conclusions drawn from such considerations enabled Holmes to reject the conservative understanding of law as something fixed and final.

Looked at logically, "each new decision follows syllogistically from existing precedent. . . . Precedents survive in the law long after the use they once served is at an end and the reason for them forgotten. The result of following them must often be failure and confusion from the merely logical point of view."

So much for form. But what of the substance of law? Law is made by judges on "considerations of what is expedient for the community concerned. Every important principle which is developed by litigation is in fact and at bottom the result of more or less definitely understood views of public policy in the last analysis." Law, in Holmes's own words, is administered by able and experienced men who know too much to sacrifice good sense to the syllogism. This explication of early forms of liability concluded on two notable observations. One, the law "is forever adopting new principles from life at one end, and it always retains old ones from history at the other, which have not yet been absorbed or sloughed off." In so stating, Holmes was insisting on a basically pragmatic rule as applied to law. Two, "while the law does still and always, in a certain sense, measure liability by moral standards, it nevertheless, by the very necessity of its nature, is continually transmuting those standards into external or objective ones from which the actual guilt of the party concerned is wholly eliminated."[26]

Holmes began his treatment of criminal law by contending that presentment is "the child of vengeance," and this desire "imparts an opinion that its object is actually and personally to blame." But the question is whether such a standard is appropriate to contemporary society. Admitting that any such form of punishment satisfies a thirst for vengeance in some way, and that criminal law has improved only gradually, still the modern view of criminal law, Holmes thinks, must be punishment meted out to protect society from actions harmful to it and its members. Punishment is not intended to reform the criminal but to deter crime. If the prisoner pays with his body, society benefits. This social reference is of the utmost importance to Holmes's understanding of all law. In criminal matters as well as in others, "the first requirement of a sound body of law is that it should correspond with the actual feelings and demands of the community, whether right or wrong." Holmes held that the law should not encourage the passion for revenge, either in individuals or the state.[27]

Having delineated the social origins of law in matters relating to civil liability and crime, Holmes proceeds to apply the same yardstick to torts. The law of torts admittedly abounds in moral phraseology—malice, fraud, intent, negligence—all of which imply that a guilty person must have some moral shortcoming. Holmes proposed an alternate theory: that man acts at his own peril insofar as society would expect a prudent man to act and to foresee the consequences of his actions. And, inasmuch as the expectations of society change, the law itself may change accordingly. Such modifications in the expectations of society are always "politic" that is, according to public policy, or what the public would support. As Holmes wrote, "a man may have as bad a heart as he chooses, if his conduct is within the rules." In other words, the standards of the law were *external* ones.[28]

As Holmes proceeds to discuss bailments, possession, and contracts, he consistently argues in favor of the socially external standard as the determining standard. Because of the prominence of contract law in the thinking of Taft, special attention should given "Holmes on Contracts." Whereas Taft was strongly traditional, Holmes was altogether pragmatic. The common element in all contracts is a promise, Holmes was to insist. One promise may be distinguished from another. For example, I promise you one hundred bales of cotton, by the degree of the power possessed by the promisor over the event involved. But, according to Holmes, the law does not require the promisor to have any assurance that he either can or will deliver on the promise made. In the moral order it may be an obligation to promise only what one can fulfill, but not so at law. "I take it that a man may bind himself at law that any future event shall happen." By so arguing, Holmes escapes the idea that a contract is a "qualified subjugation of one will to another, a kind of limited slavery." Equally practical for contemporary social requirements, damages levied in a breach of contract were not as great as those justified in tort. Furthermore, when contracts are voided the law displays no concern with the actual state of the party's mind. "In contracts, as elsewhere [the law] must go by externals and judge parties by their conduct."[29] If there are distinctions that might account for voided contracts, these distinctions are to be "found in experience, not in logic." This observation leads back unerringly to the opening statements in *The Common Law*. Having begun his study of the common law by noting that the "felt necessities" of the time were critical to understanding the nature of law, Holmes had but to reiterate this central proposition in order to conclude that the law-making process is pragmatic.

Evidence abounds of the direct translation of theories growing out of *The Common Law* into opinions of Judge Holmes on the Massachusetts bench. There was in his judicial opinions a distrust of generalities. "We think that the case at the bar /Lorenzo v. Wirth/ (1897–1898) is not beyond our competence to decide," he wrote in a majority opinion. "The greatest danger in attempting to do so is that of being misled by ready-made generalizations, and of thinking only in phrases to which as lawyers judges have been accustomed. . . . Too broadly generalized conceptions are a constant source of fallacy."[30] And in Moran v. Dunphy (1900–1901), Holmes chides the court for "wasting time on useless generalities about the construction of statutes." It was "inexpedient and unjust to lay down a sweeping general principle." Even "truth" could work hardship in a given set of circumstances.[31] In Hemenway v. Hemenway (1883), Holmes takes the position that "the court can hardly be asked to close its eyes to the truth in order to lay down a rule which can only be justified on the grounds that it is beneficial." At times the rough edges of life marked its reality, and Holmes was not likely to be dissuaded by the prospect of "doing good."[32]

His treatment of "moral rights" was in keeping with one of the main themes of The Common Law: the externalization of law. Put plainly, because the aim of the law is not to punish sin, but rather is to prevent certain external results, the act must come pretty near to accomplishing that result before the law will notice it. This principle of externalization is forcefully illustrated in Commonwealth v. Pierce (1884–1885).[33] A physician prescribed that the clothes of a patient be kept saturated in kerosene as part of his medical treatment. The patient died and the physician was sued. The question of "moral recklessness" or the intention of the physician was his method of treatment. Holmes distinguished from recklessness according to the "external standards of what was morally reckless under circumstances known to him [the doctor] as a man of reasonable prudence." Holmes reasoned further that neither idiosyncrasy nor good intention on the physician's part could be urged in his defense, and in his concluding argument invoked the externalization standard once more.

In the 1890s a series of state laws came before the Supreme Judicial Court of Massachusetts that involved questions of management-worker conflicts. The issues are basic to employee rights in an industrial society, many of which were only then being defined at the state level. In this respect Massachusetts had already taken some initiatives, in 1887 passing an Employers' Liability Act by which it was "settled law that masters were personally bound to see that reasonable care was used to provide reasonably safe and proper machinery" in works and factories. The law stated further that the worker "himself be in exercise of due care." The 1887 law was challenged in Ryalls v. Mechanics' Mills (1889–1900).[34]

Holmes contended vigorously in its defense, content to accept the intention of the legislature as stated in the statute. In his view, expressed in a dissenting opinion, an injured employee "shall have the same right of compensation and remedies against the employer, as if he had not been an employee." Therefore the injured party had the right to sue an employer to collect damages if the latter was unwilling to comply freely with the law.

An 1891 Massachusetts statute contains the following provision: No employer could withhold wages of an employee engaged in weaving for imperfection arising from the weaving process. In *Commonwealth* v. *Perry* (1891) the law's constitutionality was appealed to the Supreme Judicial Court.[35] A majority of the court ruled that the law was unconstitutional, finding in the statute impairment of contract. In other words, the property owner had a right to use his property as he chose, including withholding of wages. Holmes expressed his dissent in the plainest of language:

> So far as it has been pointed out to me, I do not see that it interferes with the right of acquiring, possessing or protecting property any more than the laws against usury or gaming. . . . It might be urged, perhaps, that the power to make reasonable laws impliedly prohibits the making of unreasonable laws . . . still I should not be willing, or think myself authorized, to overturn legislation on that ground.

Holmes had hardly broken a social reformer's lance in the cause of labor, but his dissent revealed an unwillingness to see in every law favorable to labor's interest an assault on property rights.

This neutrality in the struggle between capital and labor faced a fresh challenge some five years later in the well-known case *Vegelahn* v. *Gunter* (1896).[36] Workers were engaged in picketing manufacturing establishments in an attempt to prevent other workers from taking employment there and thus winning certain concessions from management. The question at law was the right of the court to issue an injunction restraining the pickets. The majority of the high court found the picketing illegal and therefore an injunction appropriate. Holmes, joined by the Chief Justice, Abner Field, dissented, writing, in part:

> One of the eternal conflicts out of which life is made up is that between the effort of every man to get the most he can for his services, and that of society, disguised under the name of capital, to get his services for the least possible return. Combination on the one side is patent and powerful. Combi-

nation on the other is the necessary and desirable counterpart, if the battle is to be carried on in a fair and equal way.

Holmes was, in truth, arguing in favor of the principle of labor organizing just as capital had done, in effect decrying the double standard of social morality that was sometimes a feature of Taft's jurisprudence. Methods of unionization were central in another case, *Plant* v. *Woods* (1900).[37] Could unions recruit members from other unions under the threat of boycott and strike? The Supreme Judicial Court had issued an injunction against this activity even before it began. Again, Holmes dissented, and again he voiced his contention that "unity of organization is necessary to make the contest of labor effectual, and that societies of labor lawfully may employ in their preparation the means which they might use in the final contest." As Holmes had observed, he based such judgments on history and common sense.

During his years on the Supreme Judicial Court, Holmes had numerous opportunities to discuss the law: as a profession, in its meaning, its uses, and its limitations. He spoke to various audiences on subjects as diverse as Montesquieu and John Marshall, talks delivered at various law schools, including Northwestern and Boston universities. His work frequently appeared in the *Harvard Law Review*. Of his reflections on the law offered during the period down to 1902, two addresses stand out, "The Path of the Law" (1897) and "Law in Science and Science in Law" (1899). Coming as they did toward the close of Holmes's career as a state jurist, they constitute an important and useful summary of his jurisprudential outlook just before he was advanced to the United States Supreme Court.

"The Path of the Law" was Holmes at his most didactic, as the following passages clearly emphasize.[38] His initial purpose was to disentangle legal and moral ideas. A legal right or a legal duty is "nothing but a prediction if a man does or omits to do certain things, he will be made to suffer in this way or that way, by a judgment of the court." Holmes pleaded that no one should "misinterpret what I have to say as the language of cynicism. The law is the witness and external deposit of our moral life. Its history is the history of the moral development of the race." In order to distinguish between law and morals, Holmes advanced his oft-used image: "If you want to know the law and nothing else, you must look at it as the bad man who cares only for the material consequences which knowledge enables him to predict, and not as a good man who finds reasons for conduct . . . in the vaguer sanctions of conscience." Whereupon, in coming to an understanding of the law, he notes quite simply: "I am much of his mind"—that is, the mind of the bad man. Holmes went to say that he was using a "cynical acid" to expel morality while studying the operation of the law. Drawing on juristic experience he makes his point all the stronger by referring to the realities surrounding contracts that have given rise to contract law. Thus "nothing is more certain than that parties may be bound by a contract to things which neither of them intended, and when one does not know of the other's assent." From such a consideration, Judge Holmes was prepared to accept the limits of the law.

The next principle that he addressed was the "forces which determine law's content and growth." Here he is quick to identify a fallacy, namely, that the "only force at work in the development of law is logic." The assertion is hardly surprising in light of his opening comments in *The Common Law*. What is unexpected is his lengthy attack on the notion that includes his contention that the Anglo-American system of law cannot be "worked out like mathematics from some general maxims of conduct." Holmes was especially keen to strike out against "certainty" in legal decisions. As he put it, "certainty is generally an illusion" because it is not realized how law is open to reconsideration "upon a slight change in the habit of the public mind. No concrete proposition is self-evident." Social advantages and disadvantages, which are by definition variable, Holmes believed, must be taken into account in court rulings. This was, of course, another way of presenting his theory of externalization.

At this point the judge chose to step back in order to look at the "present condition of the law as a subject for study." Admitting that it was only the beginning of a period of philosophical reconsideration of the essence of the law, he nonetheless expressed confidence that the "new" jurisprudence would eventually be recognized as the wiser and fairer approach to justice dispensed. Avowing no intention of ignoring history and tradition, these must not be allowed to continue to dominate. "It is revolting to have no better reason for a rule of law than that it was laid down in the time of Henry IV. It is still more revolting if the grounds upon which it was laid down have vanished long since." Turning to criminal law, Holmes took up the question: In judging matters should the court consider the crime more important than the criminal? In which way will society be best served? Though the crime committed may be the most heinous of actions, the criminal, the individual who committed the crime, is the greater danger to society; therefore "he must be got rid of." In his closing statements Holmes appeared to be making a strong argument for those in the legal profession to conceive of their work less according to the norms of the past—tradition—and more in keeping with the scientific norms of the present. The development of law was a new jumping-off point with the introduction of the theory of externalization. As he said of himself: "Theory is my subject, not practical details." "Theory is the most important part of the dogma of law," he continued, "as the architect is the most important man who takes part in the building of a house. The most important improvements of the last twenty-five years are improvements in theory." In saying this, Holmes left his listeners, as he does his readers, with the firm conviction that the new theory, of which he was a leading advocate, would prevail, not because it was based on reason but because it was based on science.

By way of assessment, "The Path of the Law" may be viewed in various ways. It stands as both a gloss on *The Common Law* and an effort to compare notes with fellow legal scholars (Bigelow, Ames, Thayer, Pollock, and Maitland are all referred to in the text). In some ways it is a more precise definition of the boundary between legal and moral principles, as well as a fresh assertion of the need to utilize external standards for judging the acceptability of human conduct. It would be bold to claim there is little of substance that was new in "The Path of Law," but many of its passages do have a familiar ring. Where, then, does its importance lie? First, Holmes obviously felt the need to say what he did. Second, by bringing other legal scholars into his analysis he was able to demonstrate that his somewhat unsettling ideas were not peculiarly his. Third, he may have wanted to ward off inferences that the external standard was an invitation to cynicism about morality and law. In sum, Holmes had supplied both a rehearsal of his developing jurisprudence up to that point, and every indication that he was prepared to blaze a trail into the future of American law.

An extension of the themes found in "The Path of the Law," "Law in Science and Science in Law" appears as less ambitious in its purpose and more case-oriented—understandable because Holmes was addressing the New York State Bar Association.[39] The overall message, though, is the same in both speeches. Holmes began on a provocative note: "The law of fashion is the law of life." The intellectual fashion a hundred years before was to see the universe as the sum of its intersecting parts, merely arranged to bring about the desired impression. "In our less theological and more scientific day," Holmes said, "we explain an object by tracing the order and process of its growth and development from a starting point assumed as given." The contrast in intellectual fashion is therefore both dramatic and pregnant with meaning. At this point Judge Holmes uttered one of his famous aphorisms: "Continuity with the past is only a necessity and not a duty." Should, therefore, a legislature properly empowered pass a law undermining the rule of contracts it would be at perfect liberty to do so, "without the slightest regard to continuity with the past." It followed, then, that the law could be taken into account "simply as a great anthropological document" and study of it can reveal the "transformation of human ideas." Law, in other words, is a human invention; as such, it is subject to change in order to meet human requirements. Law is a reflection of life as it was lived and as it is lived. Law did not begin with theory; rather, theory grew out of realities. For these early realities we should look to the Romans and German tribes.

Holmes interpreted history in a way favorable to the needs of a scientific understanding of the law. "History sets us free," he said. It "enables us to make up our minds dispassionately whether the survival we are enforcing answers any new purpose when it has ceased to answer the old." History enables us "to clear away the rubbish" with rubbish the equivalent of ideas and rules no longer viable in the face of a scientific approach to law. Judges may not be very good at this because they "commonly are elderly men and are very likely to hate at sight any analysis to which they are not accustomed and which disturbs their repose of mind, than to fall in love with novelties." Yet this was what judges must deal with, Holmes held, in the age of rethinking the essential law. Judges are used to certainty in their decisions; if absolutely certain, they are more content. Holmes demurred, arguing, "in the law we only occasionally can reach an absolutely final and quantitative determination, because the worth of competing social ends . . . can not be reduced to number and accurately fixed. . . . The intensity of competing desires varies with the varying ideals of the time." This led Holmes to say, "I do not believe that the jury have any historic or a priori right to decide a standard of conduct," adding: "I have not found [juries] free from prejudices than an ordinary judge would be."

In his concluding remarks Holmes sums up his legal outlook. "The real justification of the rule of law, if there be one, is that it helps to bring about a social end which we desire." In an actual case, "The social question is which desire [of the competing desires] is stronger at the point of conflict." He continued: "I have had in mind an ultimate dependence upon science because it is finally for science to determine, so far

as it can, the relative worth of our social ends." For Oliver Wendell
Holmes, social questions were always broader than judicial ones. It fell
to the legislature to initiate responses to the social questions, and for
judges to take them into account, not according to some time-honored
formula but for the social good.

In these two addresses Holmes labored long and hard to make clear
his understanding of the growth and development of the law. It was
typical of him to want to be as explicit as possible as he explained his
convictions. But he was also well known for the trenchant phrase. As
it turns out, in a few brief sentences, which could not have taken more
than a minute or two to deliver, Holmes had already stated the kernel
of his argument. The occasion was a speech at a dinner of the Harvard
Law School Association given in June 1895 in honor of C. C. Langdell.
Holmes titled his brief remarks: "Learning and Science."[40] Here essentially is what he said:

> The law, so far as it depends of learning, is indeed, as it has been called,
> the government of the living by the dead. . . . But the present has a right
> to govern itself as far as it can. . . . I hope that the time is coming when
> this thought will bear fruit. An ideal system of law should draw its postulates
> and its legislative jurisdiction from science. . . . I feel pretty sure that the
> regiment or division that follows us will carry that flag.

Such a statement resonates not only with the ruminations of the
Metaphysical Club but with the teachings of Emerson, Uncle Waldo,
who had mentored him in his youth.

The differences between Taft's understanding of the law and its social
implications and that of Holmes are self-evident. Taft was solidly given
over to absolutes which allowed him, in his judgments, only a limited
response to social conditions, whereas his future associate on the Supreme Court had stepped forth as a leading advocate of social standards,
rarely in awe of precedents for their own sake. Yet neither jurist could
be classified as an extremist at this juncture of his career. To put the
matter obversely, each would have respected the position taken by the
other, had they confronted each other in the legal process. Their common heritage accounts for much of that, along with education, reading
in the law, and court experiences. The two men were products both of
history and of their times. That being the situation, it is especially
striking that they reacted so differently to the dominant intellectual
vibrations of the period 1870–1900. Two towering personalities may well

be the reason. Taft's acceptance of Sumnerology, as expounded by the master, was countered by Holmes's early association with the ideas of Emerson to whom the past might well be forgotten in shaping a philoso- phy for today. True, Taft was not a one-dimensional Sumnerian, nor was Holmes an uncritical Emersonian; but the indelible marks upon each of their inner beings are there.

What the next twenty years would do to alter or confirm their dispa- rate legal philosophies would be hard to predict, given their distinctly different careers. Thus, when at last they sat together on the Supreme Court in the 1920s, Taft had come aboard as a public man of parts, whereas Holmes had long been the jurist, by 1921 perhaps the most respected member of the tribunal.

3

Capital Men

IN EARLY 1900, WILLIAM HOWARD TAFT WAS CALLED TO WASHINGTON BY President McKinley. It was an unexpected summons. In his ardor for judicial advancement Taft easily led himself to believe that, as a Supreme Court opening had unexpectedly developed, his fellow Ohioan was about to offer him the prize of a high court appointment. It turned out otherwise. The position offered was that of president of the Philippine Commission, a post Taft accepted with some misgivings. Two years later Oliver Wendell Holmes was summoned, not to Washington but to Oyster Bay, Long Island. President Roosevelt wanted to meet (and vet) Holmes before he would support Senator Lodge's candidate for a court vacancy occasioned by the failing health of Justice Horace Gray. Holmes, of course, passed muster and was quickly confirmed by the Senate. He had few if any misgivings about the appointment as he began one of the memorable careers in the annals of the court.

The next two decades were a political education for Taft as he moved from civil governor of the Philippine Islands to Secretary of War, President of the United States, Kent Professor at Yale and co-chairman of the National War Labor Board. It is a long road that has no turning though. The climax of Taft's public service awaited him at the age of sixty-four when, in October 1921, he took the oath of office as chief justice. At every step along the way, from appeals judge to the chief justiceship, Taft's appointments and promotions came for no small reason because of his judicious temperament and his measured way of dealing with matters political, diplomatic, economic, and educational. In tracing Taft's triumphs and disappointments it is not surprising that his qualities as a judge were manifested in his actions as in his writings. The insurrection in the Philippines was the first and most demanding test case.

The U.S. acquisition of the Philippine Islands was one of the accidents that grew out of the Spanish-American War. Unplanned, it nonetheless might well be termed an accident waiting to happen. The 1890s witnessed an increased American interest in foreign trade as factories continued to expand production beyond the capacity of the domestic markets to absorb it. Soon there was talk of reciprocal trade regulations to make it possible for U.S.-produced goods to enter previously closed markets, not simply in Europe but in the islands and nations of the Caribbean and Central America. The lure of the China trade also served to enhance the appetite of manufacturers. Curiously, perhaps, the most overt sign of this new outlook was navalism, dating from A. T. Mahan's publication in 1890 of *The Influence of Sea Power on History*. Powerful navies had become the sign of a great power; and, toward the close of the nineteenth century, Americans were thinking of themselves in just that way. With Admiral Dewey's smashing victory over the Spanish fleet in Manila Bay in May 1898, the Philippines were seen by many as a ripening fruit ready to fall into the American basket, and a steppingstone to the China trade.

President McKinley's insistence on U.S. control of the Philippines as part of the Peace of Paris ending the Spanish-American War meant that the islands would be trading Spanish masters for American masters. Yet, like the Cubans, many Filipinos yearned to be free and independent. The result was a Filipino insurrection beginning early in 1899. There followed almost three years of bloodshed as the U.S. army, numbering 70,000 troops and often employing the harshest of tactics, struggled to put down the rebellion and pacify the country by resort to *force majeur*. Under the command of General Elwell Otis, later then General Arthur MacArthur, no quarter was given, both generals fully convinced that firepower was the answer to the problem of pacification. Meanwhile, McKinley had appointed a commission headed by Jacob Gould Schurman, president of Cornell University, to go to the islands and, based on what they saw, draw up guidelines for instituting civil government. The President needed someone to assume responsibility for implementing the Schurman Commission's report. His choice of William Howard Taft was a surprising one. McKinley knew Taft only slightly; yet he was convinced, he told Secretary of War Elihu Root, that Taft was the man for the job. However, Taft required some urging on the part of ranking officials. For one thing, he had opposed American possession of the Philippines; for another, he had little, if any, administrative experience. Nevertheless, as a lawyer and judge, Taft was well grounded in the Constitution and the law, he was a man of even temper, and he was conscious of his public duty. Aware of Taft's fondness for the judicial life, McKinley promised that, should he take the assignment and thereby launch civil rule, McKinley would name Taft to the Supreme Court if and when the opportunity presented itself during his presidency. Taft, for his part, insisted on being head of the commission—which, as the American official on the scene, would make him ultimately responsible. McKinley, seconded by Root, agreed, as both were anxious to place the generals under civilian orders. Given these conditions, it becomes somewhat more understandable why Taft's initial misgivings were overcome. The appointment could well lead to the Supreme Court, after all. On 4 July 1901, after a year as chairman of the commission, he was installed as civil governor. Events and personalities were to show Taft needed to exercise his executive authority with a fine judicial hand in order to bring about both the defeat of the rebels and control of the generals.[1]

Judge Taft arrived in Manila in June 1900, with the war threatening to drag out for some time to come as American troops continued their search-and-destroy tactics. So relentless had been the punishment dealt the insurgents, there was some hope that they would soon give up; but no one could say for sure. Before Taft could nurture that possibility into reality he had to come to grips (and terms) with General MacArthur and the military mind he personified. Until Taft arrived, the military commander had full authority in the islands. To the insurrectionists, the general was prepared to meet force with force. Once the rebellion was put down, it would be a simple matter of dictating the orders that must be obeyed. To be sure, Taft had no experience dealing with the military, much less planting the seeds of self-rule in an alien clime. Possessed of common sense and a firm commitment to the rule of law as distinct from that of military force, the new commission chair determined to establish his authority over the army, convinced that, until this was achieved, there was little he could do to commence the political education of the island people. Taft clearly believed the United States held the Philippines for the benefit of the Filipinos and was not entitled to pass a single act or approve of a single measure that did not have this benefit as its chief purpose. That was hardly the policy of the American military.[2] Yet Taft did not want to address this difference in principle head on; instead, he wisely bided his time. On September 1, 1900, under instruction from Washington, the commission was to assume a legislative function, laying down rules and regulations preparatory for civilian control. At the same time, the commission chair was to take control of all U.S. finances in the islands. The power of the purse was the power to command. Military authority was thus sharply reduced.

The hurdle imposed by the military having been cleared, Taft set about winning over the Filipinos. As they came to appreciate Taft's purpose and the peaceful means of attaining it, much of the force went out of the insurrectionary movement. Its leader, Emilio Aguinaldo, was captured in March 1901, and took an oath of allegiance the next month. At this point, the U.S. army was reduced to maintaining internal security. When Judge Taft became Governor Taft, he continued to exercise a judicious manner as he faced the real work of preparing the people for self-government. Ably assisted by his wife Nellie, he showed the way to cordial relations right from the start. Members of the leading families were made welcome at the Tafts' table; and various social affairs, musicales, dinners, dances—all aimed at promoting brotherhood and feeling of equality—became routine. The response was what Taft hoped it would be: positive and enthusiastic. After all, his instructions as stated by Secretary Root were to lay the foundations of what one day would be a self-governing territory, however remote the date of full independence.

Taft's public philosophy, of which his jurisprudence formed the centerpiece, was premised on a healthy, prosperous middle class, which in turn was made up of men of property. Upon this class fell the opportunity and responsibility of making republican rule possible. Therefore it must be won over to support the American efforts which were aimed at building the first free government in Asia. It was not only natural for the good-natured judge to welcome the landed Filipinos by means of social gatherings, it was also logical. In a society thus structured, if the native leaders were won over, then the mass of the people would follow. In pursuit of this objective—the support of the ordinary people—the governor traveled far and wide across the main parts of the island group, showing himself as a friendly man, talking to local leaders and listening to them. By 1904, probably prematurely, Taft thought it possible to call together an all-Philippine congress; in fact, it did not meet until 1907. This was a sure sign of his belief in the innate capacity of the people to learn self-rule. The Cooper Act, passed by Congress in 1902 and largely the work of Taft, became a blueprint for the growth of a workable relationship between Americans and Filipinos. The judge knew that law was the sound instrument of rule but also of change and growth. His experience as lawyer, jurist, and Solicitor General found him persuaded by the famous dictum of Oliver Wendell Holmes, Jr. That is, the life of the law in the Philippines was not logic but experience, the needs of the moment, as at the same time his understanding of the U.S. Constitution made him conscious of the limits of the legal process. For Taft, experience breathed life into the logic of the law as the task of political education went forward.

The single most perplexing problem Judge Taft had to deal with in the Philippines was the disposition of the Friars' Lands. Secretary Root was to insist that when the United States purchased the properties of the religious orders, the friars must be recalled by the Vatican. This condition, which was not fulfilled, became something of a dead letter, inasmuch as two-thirds of the friars had left their plantations, voluntarily or otherwise. Those who stayed, like the Jesuits, had not become large landholders and therefore were not identified with the land exploitation associated with the other orders. Nevertheless, it was important to the American view on the place of property in a stable society that there be formal contracts transferring land to new owners. In 1902, Taft traveled to Rome to initiate discussions centering on the sale of the lands. But negotiations dragged on long after he had broken the ground, and a settlement was not finalized until November 1903. Once under U.S. ownership, the plantations were broken up into small parcels, purchasable on easy terms. It is estimated that by 1913 there were as many as fifty thousand small landholders in the islands—a situation Taft warmly approved. These property owners would be voters, with a stake in society, which, to him, constituted an essential environment for operating a free government. Taft's fondest dreams now seemed to be realized. Yet, as late as 1912, he remained unconvinced the Filipinos could be cut from America's apron strings. Self-rule was not to be accomplished quickly, if it were to survive in a world of competing imperialist powers.

On the occasion of the assembling of the first all-Filipino congress in October 1907, President Roosevelt sent Secretary of War Taft to mark the day. It was to this assembly that the first civil governor addressed his words of praise. In his speech Taft stressed the problems that had been challenges, from the settlement of the Friars' Land dispute to the difficulty of getting sufficient capital investment committed to the islands' economy, to the failure of the U.S. congress to extend commercial privileges to certain agricultural products, to the rinderpest epidemic that wiped out two-thirds of the cattle essential to working the fields. But, he went on, these difficulties had been faced and overcome, at least to a degree. Meanwhile a civil law code had been put in effect, extending the franchise to landholders literate either in Spanish or English. Taft must have beamed with satisfaction as he described how a system of justice had come into play: an independent judiciary with both American and Filipino judges sitting together, the former aiding in its administration, the latter in the process of learning how to operate the system. In Taft's own words, it had been "productive of the greatest good and right has been sustained without fear or favor." Of all Taft's objectives when he arrived to take over the governance of the Philippine Islands, none gave him as much satisfaction as courts free of political influence where justice was expected by the people and justice was done.[3]

His chief justiceship was still years away when Taft left Manila to return to Washington and the War Department. Nevertheless, the years as civil governor foreshadowed his tenure on the Supreme Court in two significant ways. Taft had insisted on heading up the 1900 commission because he wanted to be in charge, to be answerable to no one in the islands. This same impulse prompted him to tell President Harding in 1921 that he would accept a court appointment only as chief justice. Once in office he sought to "mass the court," attempting to keep dissents to a minimum—in a word, seeking to dominate it. In the second way, Taft's activism on the court was a repetition of his involvement in Filipino affairs as he appeared before congressional committees to seek a favored basis for imports from the islanders and sought to invoke legislation intended to promote self-government, of which the Cooper Act is the best example. As he had been an administrator in 1902, so would he be one in 1922, in an altogether different milieu. It is one of the ironies of Taft's career that the administrative posts he filled, the result of the political game he found himself playing, were the source of much of his accomplishment on the Supreme Court.

Taft's appointment as Secretary of War made him a governmental head in charge of a key cabinet post. The responsibilities assigned him by President Roosevelt, articulating the President's policies relative to the balance of power in the Far East and the Caribbean, added greatly to his self-confidence. Much is made of Taft as Roosevelt's able lieutenant, ever faithful to his chief. The fact is, Taft had a mind of his own, even as he carried out in detail TR's broadly stated purposes in international affairs.[4]

Taft served as Secretary of War from 1 February 1904, until his resignation 30 June 1908. Although it was a time when war between the United States and another power was extremely unlikely, the duties of the office were nevertheless preoccupying. This was especially so because Taft took every assignment given him with the utmost seriousness. The Department continued to function to some extent as a quasi-colonial office, thus adding to the Secretary's workload. With the declining health of Secretary of State John Hay (he died in July 1905), President Roosevelt made use of Taft as a diplomatic troubleshooter. For example, he negotiated the Taft-Katsura Agreement of 1905, was dispatched to Cuba in 1906 when deep political differences between the parties involved threatened an outbreak of civil war and which Taft managed to help the Cubans avoid, and laid the groundwork for the Root-Takahira Agreement of 1908. In these various nonjudicial activities Taft drew on his legal training, his respect for law, and a growing self-confidence born of his civil governorship. During these same capital days he took the occasion to write and speak on matters of law—for example, his Cooper Union address of 1908, entitled "Labor and Capital," thereby betraying his sustained concern for law and its place in contemporary affairs. An examination of Taft's tenure at the War Department in chronological order demonstrates that he moved easily from the world of international affairs, where tact and understanding traced to his judicial temper and training were indispensable, to the world of jurisprudence, where he was always at home. Taft was, at one and the same time, a man of large affairs and a legal thinker. Taft's years in Washington were the discernible beginning of his ability to be one of the most political of chief justices and at the same time learned in the law.

Theodore Roosevelt was quick to make use of Taft's experience in dealing with the Japanese—he had twice visited that country, meeting with its highest officials—when the president dispatched him to Japan in 1905.[5] It was a precarious moment for the theory and reality of balance of power in the Far East, one of the cornerstones of Roosevelt's foreign policy. TR feared that should one or the other antagonist in the Russo-Japanese War gain a decisive victory, the Far East would be destabilized—to America's disadvantage. On the one hand, Roosevelt sought to broker a peace treaty based on compromise which would deny Japan its dream of hegemony in the western Pacific, while, on the other, offering friendly assurances of U.S. regard for Japan's position in that part of the world. As it happened, Japan appeared to have the upper hand in the conflict at the time; it would require all the skills of the American spokesman to convey his country's goodwill. Apparently, Taft struck the exactly right chord with Count Katsura, the Japanese premier with whom he dealt. The quid pro quo was a simple one: Japanese agreement to respect the American presence in the Philippine Islands, and a green light from Washington for Tokyo's control of Korea. The Secretary of War had measured the ground carefully and expertly; when Roosevelt was informed of the commitment Taft had made, he pronounced it "absolutely correct in every respect." To be sure, the Japanese saw themselves as dealing with the War Secretary of a powerful nation, with all that implied. But Taft, a civilian in his bones and always an advocate of peace, viewed himself as adjudicating possible Japanese-American counterclaims in such as way as to effect an amicable resolution of the case at hand. Given the geopolitical realities, it did not require the wisdom of a Solomon, but weighing all the facts in rendering a decision.

As one of Yale University's most distinguished alumni, Taft was invited to give the Dodge Lecture for 1906. He welcomed the opportunity to address a Yale audience which he knew would be made of many undergraduates as well as alumni and friends of the university. The first of four lectures, bearning the title "The Duties of Citizenship Viewed from the Standpoint of a Recent Graduate of a University," was clearly aimed at young men of promise, many of whom would be tomorrow's business and government leaders.[6] The address touched on a number of scattered points, yet was predicated on a philosophical unity—namely, personal freedom, which it was the purpose of government to protect and which included both the possession and the use of property. Taft quickly advanced the reason, or at least one of the reasons, for the centrality of property in people's lives: "The institution of private property with all its incidents is what has led to the accumulation of capital in the world." Capitalism measured the difference between civilization and barbarism. The material comfort it produced, Taft was to insist, created the opportunity "for the cultivation of the higher instincts of the human mind and soul." If property was to be regulated in the public interest, and he had come to believe that some such regulation was salutary for the nation, it must be carefully legislated and wisely applied. Taft took great comfort in the fact that in the United States a safe way had been determined to achieve the desired end, the public good. He was referring to political parties and party government operating under the constitution. This first lecture was largely introductory, especially so in light of "The Duties of Citizenship Viewed from the Standpoint of a Judge on the Bench."[7] Later lectures took up the problems of colonial administration and lastly, the presidency.

It was his second lecture, therefore, which revealed something of his developing legal outlook. Taft's first concern was the functioning—or, as he implied, the malfunctioning—of the jury system, especially in the courts of the Southern and Western states. As he pointed out, the

English common law considered court and jury as one. It was the jury and the judge acting together that made "an admirable tribunal." This, Taft insisted, was intended by the American constitution when it spoke of trial by jury. Behind the Secretary's thinking, it should be stressed, was his concern that juries, in suits against corporations, were often "the almoners of their charity," mulching them of large sums of money by assessing fines and awarding damages. Taft, however, was not advocating the abolition of the jury system, saying, "the great advantage of a jury trial in a popular government is that it gives the public confidence 'that justice will be done.'"

In the major portion of this address the future chief justice offered several observations that are clues to his reaction to the legal outlook of Justice Holmes. Sounding a Holmesian note, Taft asserted that laws not capable of enforcement should not be passed, for they were at variance with sound public policy which, by reason of conditions in the community, were simply unenforceable. In short, law comes from the needs of the community and should be so guided. But he took aim at those who advocated that "it is better that ninety-nine guilty men should escape than one innocent man should be punished." Taft also reflected the temper of Progressive thinking in taking issue with the contention— the pernicious idea—that the wealthy were exempt from obeying the law. Taft thought this an inversion of the law since the property owner should be more concerned with having the law enforced than those lacking a stake in society. If law was not guaranteed, property could not be protected. The Sherman Anti-trust Law, for example, must be obeyed. The courts thus were critical because adjudication was the final step in the legal process. As Taft put it forthrightly: "The Courts are the background of our civilization. The Supreme Court of the United States is the whole background of the Government."

Judging by his second Dodge lecture, William Howard Taft's well-known conservatism in administrating the law bore some new features and some modifications. If property was the basis of American civilization, law was the instrument to keep property safe, and the courts were responsible for maintaining a vigilant protection of property rights. Yet Taft recognized that law was a living phenomenon, not something inert, held fast by the past. Conservative he was, he was nevertheless aware of the needs of the people in the throes of living and the abuses perpetrated by the wealthy. Control of this conflict of class interests demanded the supremacy of the law to maintain a working relationship of all groups in society.

That same year, 1906, Taft was dispatched by President Roosevelt to Cuba, there to avert a civil war by bringing under control a dispute between the two political parties, the Moderates and the Liberals. The president, Estrado Palma, whose election in 1905 had brought charges of corruption by his Liberal opponents, asked the United States to intervene. Reluctant to do so, Roosevelt moved cautiously. Instead of troops and ships, Taft and Assistant Secretary of State Robert Bacon were ordered to Havana to survey the situation and make recommendations as to the best actions to take. Taft, working quickly and effectively to defuse tempers, brought about an air of calm. Cubans generally were in agreement that the United States should play the role of peacemaker, which made the proclamation declaring the Secretary of War the provisional governor the first step toward stabilization. Eventually, U.S. troops became involved in the peace keeping mission.

What is important here, for a further understanding of Taft's developing political and legal philosophies, is to be found in the address he delivered to the students of the National University of Havana during his stay as provisional governor.[8] Taft offered a long-term solution in his insistence that, to be a success, constitutional government must depend on capitalism. Until there was a growing middle class and men of property, self-rule would not come about. He urged the young university students in particular to engage in work that would make them well off, perhaps wealthy, so they would have that all-important stake in society. In other words, they must acquire "the mercantile spirit." What was called for "was a desire to make money, to found great enterprises, and to carry on the prosperity of this beautiful island, and young Cubans ought, most of them, to begin in business." It would be necessary, therefore, to invite foreign investment capital. Foreign capital at first, and then "the gradual acquirement of capital by industrious, enterprising, intelligent, energetic, patriotic Cubans." Taft concluded his remarks with these thoughts. "The right of property and the motivation for accumulation, next to the right of liberty, is the basis of all modern, successful civilization, and until you have the community of political influence and control which is effected by the conserving influences of property and property ownership, successful self-government is impossible." In so saying, Taft was laying out a program he wanted Cubans to implement; but, from what he learned of their temper and training, he was not at all optimistic about the future. What is certain was Taft's conviction that only in this way could basic law and order be preserved.

His message was fundamentally the same for university students, whether they were in Havana or New Haven.

As had Abraham Lincoln before his nomination for President in 1860, so William Howard Taft, in January 1908, went to the Cooper Union Institute in New York City, there to deliver an important political statement. Lincoln worried about the nation divided over the issue of slavery and brought the full force of his argumentative powers to bear on the divisive character of the slavery issue. Taft, taking up a matter hardly as dangerous to the republic as Lincoln had to deal with, nonetheless examined one of the central concerns of his era: the relationship of labor and capital in industrialized America. As has been noted in his essay, "The Right of Private Property" (1894), Taft was indignant that anyone should challenge the rightful place of property in American life. At that time labor counted for relatively little in his larger view of things that mattered most. When he did take up the labor factor in the industrial equation, he became defensive in tone. In the intervening years he was to reassess the rights of labor when weighed on the scales of social justice. The net effect was coming to an acceptance of labor as an equal partner with property in the grand design of the American socioeconomy. Coming as it did in 1908, Taft's treatment of labor and capital may be interpreted as the pronouncement of the next President of the United States. He was prepared, in other words, to keep to a Progressive agenda. It was not to be the path Theodore Roosevelt had trod; it was more narrow and more circumspect. Contrary to outward appearances (Taft never learned the art of selling himself) he had not forsaken reform, although he had given it his own definition.

In "Labor and Capital," it should be noticed, Taft deliberately put Labor first in his title, thereby showing his hand.[9] (Taft's game was bridge, not poker.) His purpose was to update his understanding of those two economic institutions which, by their rivalry, were placing considerable strain on the Constitution. The address began on a theme familiar enough: "We can hardly conceive the right of personal liberty without private property, because involved in personal liberty is the principle that one shall enjoy what his labor produces." In his earlier thinking, Taft identified enjoyment of "what his labor produces" with "those who owned the means of production [and] capital needing labor to produce anything. . . . The more capital in use the more work there is to do, and the more work there is to do the more laborers are needed. The greater requirement for laborers the better the pay per man." Taft was moved to speak of "the aggregate of capital [as] the other essential element with labor in producing anything." Not unlike arguments heard in the 1990s, Taft contended that as new machines were devised having the immediate effect of bringing unemployment to some, new industries spun off from such mechanical advances, creating many more new jobs. All this is merely to say that Taft, expectedly, remained securely capitalistic in his thinking. Continuing in this vein, he added the proposition that the capitalist was "working not only for himself but for labor and society at large." (This, incidentally, is a view of the American economy Holmes would hardly have denied, so embedded in American thinking was this capitalist axiom.) As for Taft, he gave this argument various spins; for example, he insisted that "wage earners were in effect part of the moneyed classes . . . in the sense that their interests and that of the capitalist were relatively the same in requiring an honest payment of debts." Taft repeated such arguments which, if they did nothing else, conveyed his deep-seated conservatism.

Nonetheless, the future president accepted that there were areas are labor and capital are bound to clash, that, in such matters "capital will surely have the advantage unless labor takes united action." In his own words, "how could any workingmen, dependent on each day's wages for living, dare to take a stand which might leave them without employment if they had not by small assessments accumulated a common fund for their support during such emergencies?" As was pointed out, conflicts between labor and capital were not only over wages but other terms of employment as well: hours and working conditions, especially safety regulations. As a result of organized labor's insistence in these areas, which Taft deemed right and proper, there had been significant improvements for workers in general. Factory acts would not have come into being except for pressure applied by labor organizations. Agitation prevailed where altruism would not have been able to bring about change.

Employers, Taft warned, would do well to recognize that the organization of labor-the labor unions-was a permanent condition in the industrial world. Unions had come to stay. Henceforth, managers must treat employees by being prepared to deal with labor leaders. What they had in common was the success of the business enterprise involved. Labor leaders, as with corporate leaders, could be difficult to deal with; this was to be expected. Each side must understand the attitudes of the other if disputes were to be resolved. These thoughts led Taft to discuss the use of arbitration. When adjustments could not be resolved by negotiation, "it is far better for the community at large that differences be settled by submission to an impartial tribunal and agreement to abide by its judgments." There were, he admitted, constitutional pitfalls. Given the Thirteenth Amendment, "It is a very serious question whether under our constitution a decree of a tribunal under a compulsory arbitration law could be enforced against the side of laborers." Compulsory arbitration did not then appear to be a solution. In any case, an arbitration tribunal must include representation from the community affected by the dispute because, in an advanced industrial society, the community is always adversely affected by a long-drawn-out labor-capital disagreement.

Granting that strikes were costly, labor must have the right to strike. Men have the right to leave their employment, to delegate to their leaders the power to say when to strike, the right to use persuasion toward other laborers who have been brought in to replace them. Further, it was "the business of the courts and of the police to respect these rights with the same degree of care that they respect the owners of capital in the protection of their property and their business." Public sentiment had, in Taft's opinion, begun to shift to a support of labor; but a resort to violence by labor invariably alienated the public. He could not countenance violence on the part of either labor or capital. The secondary boycott invoked special condemnation; it was "a word of evil omen and ugly origin." Nonetheless, Taft was striving to remain balanced in his judgments of the rights and wrongs of labor conflict, denouncing employers' practices of blacklisting workers as particularly reprehensible.

Inevitably, Taft felt it imperative to bring up the subject of "government by injunction." The main objection to it—that it places in the hands of the judge legislative, judicial, and executive power—Taft dismissed with the following argument. There was no real difference between a judge issuing an injunction to prevent injury from a judge reaching a verdict to punish injury, because both involved an interpretation of a law and not the invention of it. "Prevention is better than cure." But, as was typical of Taft in this address, not wanting to favor labor or capital in all things considered, he admitted that the use of the writ had often been wrong, especially when violence was merely threatened but had not occurred. Injunctions, in short, had been too readily used. To guard against this misfortune, Taft favored hearings before an injunction was pronounced, going on to suggest that a different judge hear the contempt of court proceedings than the one who had issued the court order. Yet, in cases of contempt of court, he did not favor a jury trial.

In offering his conclusion to "Labor and Capital," Taft insisted that the claims of the community take precedence over the claims of either party to a dispute; this, of course, was a thoroughly Progressive principle. The Cooper Union address clearly demonstrated that the Secretary of War, soon to be President, had retained the keenest interest in legal matters of vital importance to the nation. The administration of justice under law was of great concern, despite his absence from the bench for almost a decade and, as it turned out, for years to come. He had brought a maturity of judgment to the labor-capital conflicts that marked a gravitation away from the one-sided outlook of his early years as a judge, though even in those days he had not exhibited a totally closed mind. But, as times changed, as the progressivism of the Roosevelt administration wherein he enjoyed great respect went forward, and as his own experience in the affairs of state persuaded him, Taft, by 1908, could well be defined as a conservative Progressive in matters of both law and politics.

William Howard Taft's presidency was strongly colored by court politics. He named six new members of the Supreme Court; 45 percent of all existing federal judgeships were Taft nominees during his four years in office—all in all, a remarkable record. Regarding the chief justiceship, which was the object of his desire, the responsibility of filling that post fell to him in 1910 upon the death of Melville Fuller. Edward Douglas White got the appointment, chosen over Charles Evans Hughes. Hughes was a New York Republican with a sound reputation as a reformer; White was a Louisiana Democrat and former Confederate soldier. Hughes was 48 at the time, White, 65. Granted, neither Taft nor Roosevelt much liked Hughes who, ironically one day would succeed Taft as Chief Justice; what counted against Hughes in 1910 was his age. Not a man given to calculating, Taft nevertheless thought it likely the older White would die before Hughes. Meanwhile, the New Yorker had been named an associate justice of the court, a position he resigned in 1916 to run for the presidency. Taft was right: White died in 1921, and Hughes, who lived until 1948, was Chief Justice from 1930 to 1941. Taking a step or two back from this gamble on Taft's part, it made him appear to be playing God when he put White's name before the Senate. And the gods smiled, adding to the myth that Taft was a good Ohio man who always had his plate right side up when offices were falling.

Lawyers were also destined to take a major part in the Taft administration. Roosevelt had wanted Taft in his cabinet because he could readily turn to his Secretary of War when legal advice was called for. To TR, lawyers had their uses. But Taft, in forming his cabinet, appeared to many to have gone overboard when he chose six lawyers for his official family. Only two—George Wickersham, as attorney general, and Richard A. Ballinger, secretary of the interior—made any real contribution to the work of the administration. Wickersham, a corporate lawyer before entering the cabinet, became the scourge of Wall Street as he set about enforcing the Sherman Anti-trust Act. Seventy suits under the act were argued by the Justice Department, many more in the four years of Taft in office than had been pursued in almost eight years of the Roosevelt administration. As for Ballinger, he emerged as the storm center of the fiery controversy over conservation that drove a sharp wedge between Roosevelt and Taft.

Was it simply a matter of taste that prompted Taft to surround himself with men of the law? On the contrary, the president-elect had good reason for his appointments. As he once said: "I must get the best men. I mean by that I must get the best men with the best qualifications for the place."[10] His reasoning appeared to be sound. If more reform laws were to be drafted, laws strong enough to produce results but not so reformist as to deeply offend corporations, lawyers would be required to draft the appropriate legislation. As it turned out, Ballinger unintentionally brought Taft grief, and Wickersham, by his actions against the corporations, gave substance to the claim that Taft was indeed a conservative Progressive.

George Wickersham, the most able man in the Taft cabinet, probably was the President's most trusted adviser. All this was manifested in their close cooperation in writing the original of the Mann-Elkins Act, one of the more important regulatory laws of the Progressive era. As finally agreed upon by Congress, it gave to the Interstate Commerce Commission jurisdiction over telephone, telegraphy, cable, and wireless companies. Further, it empowered the Commission to suspend new rates, including those of railroads, pending court action, in addition to providing effective enforcement of long haul-short haul pricing practices. The act also created a federal Court of Commerce to pass on appeals arising from rate disputes. The burden of proof that rates set by the Commission were unfair was the responsibility of the carriers. Because Taft had insisted that the Court be established, he was disappointed that Congress abolished it after only three years. The substance of the Mann-Elkins Act remained on the books. It may well stand as an example of Taft's middle-ground approach to regulation of interstate activities by the federal government. Taft had been especially keen to bring the railroads under stricter control because of the "lawless spirit" he associated with them.

The President's conservative Progressivism was mirrored in his response to the three great anti-trust cases involving Standard oil, American Tobacco, and U.S. Steel, all in the year 1911. Although the suits had been initiated before Taft came to office, it was his man Wickersham who brought them to closure. Both Standard Oil and American Tobacco were found guilty of violating the provisions of the Sherman Anti-trust Act and accordingly were required to divide into so many smaller corporate units. In so saying, the Court introduced the "rule of reason," with the justices reserving to themselves by a majority vote the authority to distinguish between "reasonable" and "unreasonable" trusts and monopolies. Bigness no longer was bad per se, but it might be found unreasonable by the Court. There was immediate disagreement over the point that the rule of reason had transferred legislative power to the Court, which now, under the guise of judging "reasonableness," could legitimate or dissolve giant corporations. Taft promptly endorsed the rule-of-reason principle, saying that it strengthened the Sherman Act, such was his faith in the judicial process and those men who presided over it. If the general public viewed it otherwise because the Court was by nature conservative, the President remained unmoved. The balance of power among the three branches had been adjusted more equitably.

Prosecution of the case against U.S. Steel was to reveal still another judicial rule favored by Taft—namely, that the law must be allowed to take its course, irrespective of who might be hurt. U.S. Steel had a commanding position in the processing and marketing of steel and steel products. Part of the reason for its dominance was its acquisition of the Tennessee Coal and Iron Company in 1907, a move made possible by a peculiar set of circumstances. When in that year the New York stock market declined, posing the risk of a full-fledged crash and possible depression to follow, the steel giant took advantage of the uncertainty obtaining in the business world to tender an offer for the Tennessee firm. Supposedly this purchase would have a steadying effect on the market and bad times could be avoided. But there was apprehension on the part of the steel magnates that the acquisition would violate the Sherman Anti-trust Act. To guard against this, President Roosevelt was sounded out. Because he entered no objection to the deal, U.S. Steel's purchase of the smaller company went forward. The financial crisis passed, and Roosevelt was content, until his action inevitably came under the scrutiny of Taft's man, Wickersham. The more the latter dug

into the facts of the case against U.S. Steel, the more it appeared that
Roosevelt had allowed himself to be duped by the Wall Streeters. At
this point in the proceedings, President Taft might well have ordered
Wickersham to avoid embarrassing his old friend, skirting the issue of
Roosevelt's involvement which in fact was hardly crucial to the prosecution's case. But Taft chose not to intervene, much to Roosevelt's chagrin. It is unlikely that the President enjoyed TR's discomfort, but he
believed that the judicial process should play favorites with no man.
Roosevelt countered by revealing that Taft himself had approved of the
deal as it was being made. The President did not attempt to exempt
himself from blame, in keeping with his determination that all the facts
should be made public. Wickersham won his case against the steel monopoly and the law was upheld—which, to Taft, were the important
considerations.[11]

No one before him coming into the presidency had as wide experience
in dealing with non-American nations and peoples as did William Howard Taft. Not the Adamses, not Thomas Jefferson, widely traveled as he
was in France and Italy, came close to Taft's knowledge of differences
in the human race: Filipinos, Japanese, Cubans, denizens of the Vatican.
His work as governor, diplomat, and troubleshooter had a shaping effect
on one particular aspect of his jurisprudence, not to mention the influences on his policies as President. The effort to negotiate a treaty of
commercial reciprocity involving Canada is a good example of his maturing view of international cooperation as part of America's *weltpolitik*.
Far more ambitious, and more farsighted as well, was Taft's attempt to
arrange treaties of arbitration with Great Britain and France and, possibly, other great powers. He once said to his military aide, Major Archie
Butt, a genuine treaty of arbitration would be "the great jewel of my
administration . . . it will also be the greatest failure if I do not get it
ratified."[12] Such a statement speaks volumes for Taft's faith in arbitration;
possibly it was a new and effective branch of international law. He was
encouraged by the work of the Courts of International Justice at The
Hague, the veriest beginnings of a system whereby lawyers would argue
cases and judges would hand down decisions with no thought of going
to war. Taft came to believe that there should be no nonjusticiable issues
between nations. Addressing a meeting of the American Arbitration
and Peace League in 1912, he announced that "personally I don't see
any more reason why matters of national honor should not be referred
to a court of arbitration any more than a matter of property or national
proprietorship."[13] As president he was especially hopeful Great Britain

and France would be responsive to American initiatives and received encouragement from Sir Edward Grey, the British Foreign Secretary, Lord James Bryce, HM Ambassador to the United States, and from Jules Jussernad, the French envoy to Washington. To someone of Taft's temperament and training, the prospect of international law requiring arbitration fitted well with the inner man and his judicial mind. When Taft presented treaties seeking to establish the practice of arbitration to the U.S. Senate, he was astonished and ashamed that his basic idea had been totally rejected. He simply refused to send the Senate version of the treaties to either London or Paris, where, he thought, they would have been viewed as either foolish or treacherous. Responding at home to this Senate action, Taft insisted that opposition to arbitration "cannot be found in the constitution . . . it must be construed from it." His grand design, in which courts of international justice would usher in an era of peace and harmony, died the death in the Senate, and soon thereafter in the Great War. Something of its spirit lived on in Taft's efforts to prepare for a workable peace once the war to end all wars was over. In the spring of 1915, the former President of the United States was elected president of the American Association for the Judicial Settlement of International Disputes. Along with such leaders as A. Lawrence Lowell, president of Harvard, and Henry S. Prichett, head of the Carnegie Endowment, Taft was convinced that, once attained, peace could be preserved only by nations making common cause against rogue nations, using force if need be. He was not a "peace at any price" man; as in any workable system of law, behind the books of the law stood the sword of justice.

An examination of Taft's writings when he was a member of the Yale faculty, the years 1913–1917, may well be described as revealing a period of calm reflection on the nature of American constitutional government and a willingness on his part to "go public" as he assessed past history, current developments, and future probabilities. At no place in his writings can be discovered the probability of his becoming chief justice; he was too familiar with the realities of "luck of the draw" when it came to such a prospect. Indeed, we should recall that Taft had calculated that Edward Douglas White would die before Charles Evans Hughes. But, given the twists and turns of fate, he was much more interested during his years at Yale in speaking his mind—in such writings as *Popular Government* (1913), *The Anti-Trust Act and the Supreme Court* (1914), *The United States and the Peace* (1914), and *The President and His Powers* (1916)—than anticipating a high court appointment. Nonetheless, his books provide insight into the evolution of Taft's judicial mind, while, on occasion, anticipating certain of his Court opinions in the 1920s. No account of his preparation for the chief justiceship can afford to ignore the reflective Taft; his admiration for John Marshall, for example; his generous interpretation of presidential powers, especially in foreign affairs; and a steadfast conviction of the rightful place and real power of the Supreme Court in the governance of the American people.

Taft's appointment at Yale called for him to teach a course on the Constitution. As he took up residence well after the start of term, he chose instead to deliver a series of lectures on the Constitution, eight in number, using the Preamble as his text. These lectures, combined with two other addresses, make up the content of *Popular Government*. [14] Taft's constitutional conservatism was immediately apparent. He held that popular government—identified particularly by the cry for the use of initiative, referendum, and recall—was at variance with the entire thrust of the Constitution as it was conceived by the Founding Fathers. Such innovations seemed to say to him that the system was faulty, a proposition Taft vehemently denied. Like Marshall, he favored a certain remoteness of government from the mass of voters. The authority of the Supreme Court had to remain free of popular and impractical fads, however sincere the intentions of their proponents. He quoted Blackstone and James Wilson to this effect: "a certain number of men might assume to act in the name of the community." The highest form of rule was representative, republican government and not mass action which he found often fickle and possibly dangerous. This was part of the genius of the historic document; the system required no improvement. The system not being at fault, it sometimes occurred that the people used the system improperly. Not surprisingly, Charles A. Beard's thesis, as presented in *Economic Origins of the Constitution*, Taft dismissed out of hand. And he quoted approvingly from his veto message respecting Arizona's initial petition to be admitted into the Union. In particular, Taft objected to a provision for the recall of judges, one of the provisions of the territorial constitution. Finally, in *Popular Government*, Taft made clear why he objected to the "new devices" being put forward by reformers. They eliminated "all distinction between a constitution as fundamental law and statutes enacted for the disposition of current matters." His argument continued: "When exactly the same sanction is given to a statute as to a constitution, to an appropriation bill and a bill of rights so that one may be repealed as easily as the other, the peculiar office of the constitution ceases to be." For Taft, there could be no retreat from this position.

In the former president's judgment the Sherman Anti-Trust Act in 1890, as implemented by the rule of reason in 1911, were the perfect complement giving the federal government the means to curb the abuses of the public interests by the trusts. He was therefore middle of the road, but well to the right of the exact center. He took a dim view of the Clayton Anti-Trust Act because of the mischief it might do to legitimate, albeit large, corporations. In what was Taft's most scholarly piece of writing, *The Anti-Trust Act and the Supreme Court*, he thought it useful to delve into English common law at the time of Henry V, where he discovered an early reference to freedom from restraint of trade.[15] On the other hand, in the England of a later date, monopolies, especially in foodstuffs, were condemned under the law. In other words, trade might be regulated if the community interest required it. In addressing the Sherman Act, Taft drew on authorities, including Holmes and Frederic Maitland, to show that the laws respecting freedom of trade must change in response to new conditions. Taft termed this "moral progress" in the law. The enormous changes that took place in the American socioeconomy from 1870 to 1890 required action on the part of Congress if the public good was to be served. Under the Constitution, the Supreme Court had the ultimate responsibility for determining the law as good or bad. It was this set of circumstances that called for "judicial guidance" with the High Court as the appropriate institution to pass judgment. Taft accepted changes in he law, provided the justices had the final say. In fact, the Court itself should move with the times. As Taft noted, if *Lochner* v. *New York* had come before the Court in 1913, rather than 1906, the outcome would have been different. But it was an earlier government suit against a monopoly, the *E. C. Knight Case*, that provided Taft with an opportunity to explore the applicability of the Sherman Act. He quoted at length from Chief Justice Fuller's majority opinion rejecting the government plea to enforce the Sherman law, as well as from Justice Harlan's dissent. But Taft appeared to dodge the bullet when he argued that the outcome of the suit rested on the inadequate preparation of the government's briefs. In the last analysis, Taft was led back to English common law practice. By approving the Court's action in the Standard Oil and American Tobacco cases of 1911, he insisted that the justices were in the best—that is, most objective— position to determine whether or not a trust was reasonable. By invoking the rule of reason the Court was "merely following a common law standard."

As war clouds gathered over Europe—the Balkan Wars of 1912–1913 appeared to portend a greater war—Taft took up the cause of peace. Four lectures given at the New York Peace Society during the winter of 1913–1914 were published in book form the year World War I began. Especially pertinent to Taft's commitment to some form of international law was his plea for "arbitration treaties that mean something." Part of his argument was that binding arbitration was "no new thing" in American law, being well within the treaty-making power granted by the Constitution. Arbitration would be greatly facilitated by a permanent association of nations. Once the arbitration process was joined to an international organization, a framework would exist for courts and judges to take up the charge of deciding disputes on the merits of each case. Here again, Taft revealed his almost boundless faith in the efficacy of the judicial process.

The President and His Powers was Taft's most widely discussed book published during his years at Yale—and with good reason.[16] Under Theodore Roosevelt, and under Taft himself, the office had taken on much greater importance than in previous administrations, and people wanted to know what a former president, a man who had "been there," had to say. Following are some of the points he made regarding past and future occupants of the White House, which showed a judicial face. In considering the President's veto power, Taft urged that presidents reject any bill passed by Congress which the chief executive believed was unconstitutional. The Constitution must be protected from assault at every step in the legal process. In the conduct of diplomacy, Taft proposed allowing presidents a great deal of discretion. He likened his use of troops in Nicaragua to President Cleveland's resort to the injunction at the time of the Pullman strike; it seems that his mind invariably displayed a preference for judicial comparisons. As for the nature and scope of executive power, Taft found in the Constitution the source of impressive executive authority, adding that the Supreme Court rarely sought to rein in presidents. Not that he accepted Theodore Roosevelt's "residuum of power" thesis. According to Roosevelt, any power not legislative or judicial that governments enjoy must, by process of elimination, devolve upon the President. In so saying, Taft was as prepared to castigate a Thomas Jefferson or a Theodore Roosevelt. Furthermore, it was the duty of judges—above all other officials, and perhaps above all men—to guard against abuses of power.

The last public service Taft performed before his appointment to the Supreme Court was as co-chairman of the National War Labor Board. The NWLB has been termed "the Supreme Court of Labor Relations," a way of assessing its character and importance, which no doubt would have pleased Taft. Occasioned by the exigencies of wartime industrial production, it was a board very much Progressive in form and purpose. Acting for the nation, the Wilson administration sought to maximize the output of war material, and to orchestrate capital and labor in such fashion as to achieve that objective. But the economy, of course, remained a capitalist one, which meant that the owners and workers would more than likely see matters in a different light when it came to wages, hours, and working conditions. When it came to a labor dispute, each side sought to use the common cause of winning the war as leverage against the other. In order to prevent costly work stoppages, President Wilson, in April 1917, created the NWLB to arbitrate the conflicting demands of owners and workers. The interests of business and trade unionist were equally represented on the ten-man board. Frank P. Walsh, a union organizer, joined William Howard Taft, a former president viewed as sympathetic to capital, to head up the Board. During its fourteen months of operation the NWLB heard more than 1,200 cases involving some 700,000 workers. The Board's contribution to the war effort was an important factor in maintaining industrial output, which, in turn, had significant influence on the outcome of the conflict.[17]

To be sure, Taft, as a former judge, was thoroughly familiar with judicial procedure and the work of a Court. At the NWLB, however, he would face problems he had little knowledge of from prior experience. It was, once again, a matter of on-the-job training, much as it had been when Taft went on the Superior Court of Ohio, at which time he remarked that he learned to be a judge at the taxpayer's expense. Now he again threw himself into the learning process; the very first month, he went into the South to apprise himself of working conditions in the mills and factories there. It was an eye-opener, as Taft saw first-hand the realities of industrial labor, and he was appalled. So troubled was he that he ordered an immediate increase in pay, in some instances tripling the wage scale, so that the workers could enjoy a decent standard of living. It is interesting to contrast the willingness of Taft to educate himself in a hands-on kind of way with Oliver Wendell Holmes who on occasion refused an invitation from Justice Brandeis to visit what Holmes must have known were "dark, satanic mills." Taft, in fact, turned out to be a champion of labor, supporting the right of unions to organize in opposition to the owners, the eight-hour day, and a living wage for all workers, including "the common laborer."

Despite the disparity in their backgrounds and outlook, Taft and Walsh worked as a team as they looked into the causes of strikes, called or pending, and found for the workers. Walsh was flamboyant, Taft acted with judicial calm. In the investigation of Smith & Wesson, an important manufacturer of arms, Walsh denounced the company in typical trade union invective while Loyall Osborne, another Board member, was the shrill voice of the employers. Taft's style made him appear the moderate, yet one who favored labor. Furthermore, as a former President of the United States, Taft was able to impart to the Board and its undertakings a much greater respect than would otherwise have been the case. As was to be true of his work as Chief Justice, Taft was master of the detail of cases as they came before the Board, convinced that only by knowing the facts could fair judgments be rendered. To some, Taft had become a radical; but, in his own view, he was merely doing a job that needed to be done. No doubt he had a certain zest for his Board position because it brought him back to Washington where he felt he was making a contribution to the war effort, no small matter for a man of Taft's patriotic impulses. With the war ending in November 1918, the NWLB would soon be folding its tent, which meant that, for the moment, his future course was uncharted.

He was in his early sixties, in good if not robust health, and as ready as ever to serve his country, whether as a spokesman for world peace, a cause in which he deeply believed, or in some other capacity in public or private life. The next presidential election was two years away, and the Republican Party might or might not return to the White House. Taft was still a good Ohio man; but whether important office might again come his way would depend on the will of the people—people, that is, who wielded power.

Meanwhile, Taft continued to think and speak his mind in matters of jurisprudence. In 1921, he accepted an invitation to deliver the Cutler Lecture at the University of Rochester. The address, titled "Liberty Under Law," found Taft reiterating two fundamental principles he thought appropriate to emphasize at the time.[18] The first of these he stated as follows: Our Constitution "rests on personal liberty and the right of property. In the last analysis personal liberty includes the right of contract and the right of labor." In Taft's mind, property was the right of the worker to enjoy what he earns and the right of owners of property to look after their interests. Balancing the two, each with due regard for the right of the other, was the one true guarantee of material progress. Taft's second principle, maintaining a representative form of government whereby the will of the electorate was refined by legislative action, he cast in negative terms. He again attacked the "adoption of the so called 'purer' democracy" represented by such devices as the initiative, referendum, and recall; he also advanced arguments against the open primary as part of the same kind of unwise tinkering with the method of governing. Such primaries would bring about the destruction of party responsibility, question the fitness of candidates, and weaken party discipline. Furthermore, what would happen to the party platform if the conventions were no longer to meet? In the same lecture, Taft recognized that government action was sometimes critical to progress, but that there was "only a limited zone within which legislation and government can accomplish good." "Liberty Under Law" was both a reminder that Taft had made an effort to equate the rights of labor and of capital by placing each under the protective mantle of property and insistence on a limit to what the people could rightly expect the government to do for them. Whatever the future might hold for Taft, he was certain to continue to be a legal theorist whose outlook would be influenced by what he had come to know about the working of the law on a day-to-day basis.

Oliver Wendell Holmes became a capital man when, in 1902, he was sworn in as an associate justice of the Supreme Court of the United States. Soon thereafter, he wrote to his British friend, the legal scholar, Sir Frederick Pollock. He was in a rare euphoric mood. Regarding his work, Holmes was "more absorbed, interested, and impressed than ever I dreamed I might be."[19] His earlier court endeavors seemed "a finished book—locked up far away, and a new and solemn volume opens." He was struck by "the variety and novelty of the questions, the remote spaces from which they came, and the amount of work they require." Holmes was a truly happy man as he threw himself into meeting his new responsibilities.

The appointment of Holmes as a justice was not, however, written in the stars. The position might have gone to another except for his friendship with Henry Cabot Lodge and in turn Lodge's friendship with Theodore Roosevelt. In February 1902, Justice Horace Gray, a Massachusetts man, had fallen ill. Because of the seriousness of his condition, and considering his age, it was doubtful that he would be able to return to his post. The tradition that the Court should always have a Massachusetts member was well established, so that both George F. Hoar and

Henry Cabot Lodge, the junior of the two senators from Massachusetts, became keenly interested in the choice of Gray's successor. Hoar had the advantage of senatorial seniority, offset by Lodge's close association with the President. Lodge went on the offensive almost at once, pushing the Holmes candidacy with TR as befit their friendship. There were other aspirants—William H. Moody, then Secretary of Navy, and Samuel Hoar, a nephew of Senator Hoar—which heightened the personal nature of the competition. Lodge stole a march on his senate rival in coming out strongly for Holmes in his frequent, private conversations with Roosevelt.

In addition to Lodge's support there was much about Holmes to recommend him to the President. He was of distinguished lineage, his Civil War record was brilliant, and his apparently pro-labor rulings while on the Massachusetts high court all appealed to Roosevelt. Yet he hesitated, having taken offense at what Holmes had said in estimating the historical importance of Chief Justice John Marshall. To TR, Marshall was a hero because the latter was a fierce nationalist and saw fit to interpret the Constitution in exactly that way. Taft felt much the same, pronouncing Marshall the greatest American jurist, if not the greatest of all public men, in the nation's history. Holmes, for his part, was not so sure. In his Marshall Day Address—given in 1901 to mark the one hundredth anniversary of Marshall taking charge of the Supreme Court— he expressed his reservations. "I should feel a doubt about whether, after Hamilton and the Constitution itself, Marshall's work proved more than a steady intellect, a good style, personal authority in his court, courage, justice, and the convictions of his party."[20] An incensed Roosevelt had to be reassured by Lodge that Holmes did indeed believe in the principles of the Republican party, that he was a good party man. Only after meeting personally but informally with Holmes—not at the White House, but at Sagamore Hill—was the President ready to send his name to the Senate for confirmation. In the long view, despite the breach in their friendship following Holmes's dissent in the *Northern Securities* case of 1904, Roosevelt would have small reason to regret his choice.

Was Holmes, then, a Progressive jurist or, to cast the question in more general terms, was he liberal or conservative? Supreme Court justices are frequently labeled as liberal or conservative by those who, for whatever reason and from whatever perspective, seek to separate the sheep from the goats. For most of the High Court in this century, it may be generally said that for the justices, as for public men at large, "liberal" and "conservative" labels have had political and socioeconomic meanings. These have been determined by certain preconceptions about the nature of man and the rights which are preserved to mankind, as well as by reference to the place of government in people's lives. As such terms were used at the start of the twentieth century, political liberalism placed great emphasis on natural rights and civil rights, conservatism on natural duties and civic duty. Liberals favored an increased governmental power exercised by officials genuinely representative of the people. Conservatives suspicious of big government, wanted such public power as there was placed, in the hands of officials of the utmost probity. In socioeconomic matters, liberalism demanded an increased share by the workers in the fruits of capitalism and protection of the workers and the public in general from abuses arising from laissez-faire. Conservatives approached socioeconomic issues in a spirit of individualism which government had the duty to foster. For different reasons and with different points of emphasis, American liberals and conservatives of the era were optimistic and confident. They recognized the innate dignity of men and women. They expected government to protect the rights of all citizen. And they looked to a better day.

By reference to such standards, it is easier to place Taft in the political, and thus judicial, spectrum than it is Holmes. Taft was to the right of center but not so far right as to ignore the social and economic inequities common to the nation and to want to alleviate them, insofar as it was constitutionally possible. Accordingly, it is correct to identify him as at times progressive—for example, his support of the Mann-Elkins Act of 1910, his call for a unified budget for the federal government, and, at a different level, his enthusiasm for a postal savings bank for the benefit of the working class. Holmes, in contrast, presents a more complex set of ideas regarding government and the socioeconomic order. Was he neither liberal nor conservative, but only Holmesian? Perhaps that is to equivocate. Another label that may prove a better fit is that of "coincidental Progressive." The first twenty years of this century saw the high tide of Progressivism, only to have it recede with the coming of World War I, and Holmes was often Progressive in his court opinions.

The first twenty years of Holmes on the Supreme Court may be usefully divided into two unequal time periods. From 1902 to 1917, the Court was preoccupied by cases growing out of legislation spawned by rapid changes in American life at nearly all levels. With the coming of the war, cases arising from the nation arming itself became the pressing business before the justices. Whether in voting with the majority or writing opinions in dissent, an increasingly active Holmes had an influential voice in the Court's deliberations and judgments. During these same years, as his correspondence reveals, he cultivated and was cultivated by numerous people of rank and distinction. He made trips to the British Isles, gave addresses in various American cities, and did the occasional piece for the *Harvard Law Review*. All such activities were but distractions from his main concern, the business of the Supreme Court. Only after considering the most important rulings handed down by the justice during the Progressive years and its analog, American involvement in World War I, is it possible to offer a judgment whether Holmes was liberal or conservative, coincidentally Progressive or merely Holmesian. In any final analysis of Holmes's judicial philosophy, an unequivocal assertion as to its character may not be determined, nor may it be any less understood in consequence.[21]

As absorbed as the new justice became in his work, the nature and number of cases the Court heard and ruled on were nearly always an outgrowth of the increasingly complex socioeconomy of the nation. By studying cases at hand, by drawing on his state court experience, and by occasionallly relying on intuition, Holmes was rarely long or far away from the public realities, conditions unimaginable to the Founding Fathers or to the pre-Civil War generation. A point of law in a given case might hinge on some abstruse technicality, but the court's rulings invariably had an impact on how business was conducted or on the interests of the consumer or what constitutional corner had been turned. This was the living law the Court must decide whenever it came to content and direction. Due to economic and social disputes carried over from the late nineteenth century or because of innovative reform laws passed by Congress and enforced by successive administrations, Holmes and his colleagues were continually immersed in public affairs, deciding issues, raising questions, and advancing new interpretations of constitutional law. Holmes was very much in his element. Years before, he had vacated the Weld Professorship at the Harvard Law School in favor of becoming a Massachusetts commonwealth judge. By temperament, he much preferred action to observation, the bench to the lecture hall. For Holmes, better the judicial arena than the scholar's closet; yet, as he wrestled with the facts of a case and how they should be related to the law which must be obeyed, he remained a scholar.

An examination of a number of Holmes's opinions, written in agreement with the Court majority or in dissent, opinions representing the full range of his legal philosophy as it had developed down to 1921, occasions several general observations. New in his job, Holmes first had to learn Court protocol; despite his twenty years experience as a state jurist, he began as much an apprentice as he was an associate justice. To be sure, he was a quick and confident learner, eager to meet his responsibilities; but learn he must. He was hardly the "great panjandrum of the law" he later became. Second, cases he was to study and decide on enabled him to feature these aspects of legal realism that eventually became his hallmark. But growth in this direction was to be a measured one. Third, Holmes would have the opportunity to test his theoretical understanding of the proper relationship between the political branches of government: legislative, executive, and judiciary. This was to eventuate in a great respect for the will of legislatures, both state and federal. Fourth, Holmes responded in definite ways to the temper of the times, aptly illustrated by his position in cases dealing with civil liberties during World War I. Finally, it was only in his late years that the honorable justice became the "venerable" justice. In the real world, men must climb the heights of Mount Olympus; they are not born there. To sum up and state the foregoing observations simply, Holmes's Supreme Court career must be read forward from its starting point, not backward from its climax. The very first case in which he participated, Otis v. Parker (1903) serves to illustrate certain of the foregoing postulations.[22]

Otis v. Parker involved a law passed by the California legislature which forbade buying stocks of any corporation on margin. The legislation was intended to police the securities industry in the state as protection against financial disaster. Challenge to the law was based on the idea of personal liberty guaranteed against state interference by the Fourteenth Amendment. Did the word liberty include contracts for this kind of stock purchases? Holmes identified two important considerations, liberty of contract and the police power of the states, as being in conflict. The case offered him the opportunity to apply the rule that the law is what judges say it is. Echoing the sentiments of John Marshall, in McCullough v. Maryland (1819), that this was a constitution the Court interpreted, and not a code of law, he came down on the side of the state of California, particularly its legislature, whose police power was subsumed by the Tenth Amendment. By taking into account the benefit to the community, as opposed to the rights of individuals, Holmes argued that society, by being better served, deserved the protection of the law. This deference to the legislature, though not always adhered to, bespoke Holmes's respect for those who make the laws even when they are foolish laws. As he later said to John W. Davis regarding the Sherman Anti-Trust Act, "Of course I know and every other sensible man knows that the

Sherman Law is damned nonsense, but if my country wants to go to hell, I am here to help it." It took one of the justice's most fervent admirers, Francis Biddle, to point out that Holmes could "for the sake of the *bon mot* or neat aphorism let out the most absurd generalities as if they were self-evident truths." In light of the foregoing remarks, Holmes's stated position in the Northern Securities case may not be surprising, but it was unexpected, and this is the more important historical consideration. He had, after all, given a different signal in certain of his Massachusetts opinions.

The Northern Securities case had all the earmarks of a political move by Theodore Roosevelt as he began preparations for the next presidential election.[23] He directed Attorney General Olney to bring suit against the giant holding company for violating the Sherman Act, an early instance of TR's trust-busting. By 1904, the case had moved from the federal district court in St. Paul, Minnesota, to the Supreme Court, with the government winning in a five-to-four decision. Much to the chagrin of President Roosevelt, if not that of Senator Lodge, Holmes voted against the government. His dissent was deemed "conservative" at the time. Furthermore, by challenging the constitutional wisdom of the national legislature, it appeared to be a piece of judicial activism.

Justice Holmes began his critique by noting that "great cases, like hard cases, make bad law." The statute in question was a criminal statute, and Holmes could discern no criminal action. "Again the statute is of very general and sweeping character. It hits 'every' contract or combination . . . great or small, and 'every' person who shall monopolize or attempt to monopolize . . . 'any part' of the trade and commerce among the states." The wording was simply too all-embracing. To Holmes, the facts of the case were such that the Sherman Act could not be applied because he could discern neither contract nor combination in restraint of trade, in passing observing that the idea of "preventing" competition was not found in the words used in the law. Holmes believed that the exact wording of the law bound him to interpret only the words, not some supposition of the lawmakers fifteen years earlier. Holmes did not view himself as being "conservative" but as being literal, and thus realistic. To buttress his argument, he appealed to evolutionary forces at work in society. The effort of the railroad magnates in forming the Northern Securities Corporation, he saw as part of the operation of that natural law. In such ways did society grow and progress as the railroad services could be made more efficient through combination. There is a trace of an Olympian stance in this reasoning; but there is also to be found more than a trace of Holmes's abhorrence of absolutes. The emphasis he placed on the word *every* in every combination, contract, or person should be decoded to read *absolute* prohibition of contract and combination. This he found intellectually unacceptable and, from a legal perspective, unconstitutional, given the facts of the Northern Securities case. Whether conservative, realistic, or Holmesian, the year 1904 is too early in his career on the Supreme Court to be used in determining his reputation.

Holmes's dissent in *Lochner v. New York* (1905) and his majority opinion in *Swift and Company v. United States* (1905) both of which followed closely on the heels of the *Northern Securities* case, served notice on Roosevelt, Lodge, or anyone else that he would be predictably unpredictable.[24] The Lochner case had to do with the constitutionality of a New York State law which placed a limitation on the number of hours per day and per week a baker might be employed in a bakery. The state had exercised its police power in such a regulation, contending that maximum hours were related to the health of the bakers as well as the health of the consuming public. The law clashed immediately with the economic liberty of bakery owners to use their property in whatever manner they saw fit. In a five-to-four decision, the Supreme Court ruled against the state statute. Mr. Justice Peckham, for the majority, found that the state had engaged in "meddlesome interference" with the right to purchase or sell labor as guaranteed by the due process clause of the Fourteenth Amendment, asserting that the law looked like regulation of hours for its own sake and had nothing to do with the health of the bakers involved. Holmes wrote a separate, dissenting judgment that centered on five specific points: (1) the case was decided upon an economic theory which a large part of the country did not entertain; (2) it is settled that state laws may regulate life in many ways which legislators might think injudicious; (3) "General propositions do not decide case. The decision will depend on a judgment or intuition more subtle than any articulate major premise"; (4) the word *liberty* in the Fourteenth Amendment was perverted if it worked to obstruct the natural result, unless it could be said that a rational and fair person would admit, of necessity, that the law at issue would infringe fundamental principles; and (5) "A reasonable man might think [the New York law] a proper measure on the score of health." This dissenting opinion, containing as it did so much of the essence of Holmes's judicial thinking, has become a classic expression of his legal philosophy.

Swift and Company v. United States marked another victory in the

Roosevelt administration's attack on the trusts.[25] Suitably enough, Holmes spoke for the majority in affirming the decree of a circuit court which had enjoined the meatpacking firm from engaging in unlawful restraints and monopolies. Swift and Company controlled more than half the trade and commerce in fresh meats among the states. The bill of particulars alleged against the company was impressive. It charged that a combination of dealers in fresh meat throughout the country had agreed not to bid against each other in the livestock markets of the several states, to bid up prices for a few days to encourage cattlemen to send stock to the stock yards, to fix prices at which they would sell, to restrict shipments to maintain prices, to keep a blacklist of noncooperating dealers, and to arrange rebates to railroads. The intent of all these activities, it was charged, was "to monopolize and to prevent competition." Counsel for Swift answered that the charges did not set forth "sufficient definite or specific facts." Holmes's response for the Court showed his disposition to "nicely analyze" the legal problems in the case. He wrote in part: "The scheme is so vast that it presents a new problem in pleading. . . . Its size makes the violation of the law more conspicuous, and yet the same thing makes it impossible to fasten the principal fact to a certain time and place." Nonetheless, Holmes concluded, "The scheme as a whole seems to us to be within reach of the law. The constituent elements are enough to give the scheme a body and, for all that we can say, to accomplish it. Moreover, whatever we may think of them separately when we take them up as distinct charges, they are alleged sufficiently as elements of the scheme." Beyond these considerations, Holmes also discerned from the facts in the case a clear illustration of "stream of commerce," one of the important derivative concepts of the Constitution's commerce clause.

This argument in the Swift and Company case in support of antitrust action was as thorough and finely reasoned as was Holmes's dissent in the Northern Securities case, in which Holmes had reached an opposite conclusion. What may be said to account for his contrary interpretations in the two cases? Several different factors, especially if taken in combination, add up to an explanation. The physical evidence of the manipulation of prices by the Swift company agents is one such factor. The tangible impact of combination is another. The vastness of the scheme itself implying as it did a deliberate plan, seems also to have been persuasive. Finally, the very subject in the dispute—the shipment of food, a necessity of life—should be taken into account. If Holmes was prepared to judge a case on its merits, and not according to some generalized formula, the facts in *Swift and Company* v. *United States* were such as to convince him of the constitutionality of this particular regulation of a trust in the public interest.

Holmes's predilection for dissent blossomed within three years of his coming on the Court. Whether his views laid down guidelines, marking out a future growth of the law, remained to be seen. Though reasonably sure that his interpretations were sound law, he did not insist on their dogmatic certainty. In *Missouri* v. *Illinois* (1905), for example, Holmes disagreed with the majority, which held that sewage entering the Mississippi River in Illinois made that state accountable for the evil effects of contaminated water downstream in Missouri.[26] In a confrontation between two states, where the evidence presented by plaintiff and defendant appeared equally strong, Holmes declined to take sides. In *Haddock* v. *Haddock* (1905), he dissented because he discerned further encroachments by the Court on state sovereignty in a suit involving divorce laws in New York and Connecticut.[27] "I do not suppose that civilization will come to an end which ever way this case is decided," Holmes admitted; but he foresaw unnecessary mischief for innocent parties when state divorce laws were interfered with. Offering still another dissent in *Carroll* v. *Greenwich Insurance Company* (1905), in which Holmes held constitutional an Iowa law which forbade fire insurance companies doing business in the state from agreeing on rates, the need for judicial restraint came through as a paramount consideration in his reasoning.[28] In *Ellis* v. *United States* (1906), Holmes came to the defense of the eight-hour day for laborers and mechanics in a U.S. Navy shipyard.[29] The workmen party to the suit had been hired by a private contractor, a fact which the majority of the Court deemed adequate reason to suspend the eight-hour limitation on government employees. Such interpretations may be regarded as leading toward two of the more widely heralded of Holmes's dissents which hewed to the Progressive line: *Adair* v. *United States* (1908) and the First Employers' Liability cases (1908).[30] An examination of these cases and the Holmesian response to them may be especially helpful for seeing through to the center of his impulse to dissent. Whether or not Holmes's departure from the Court majority made him a judicial prophet, no one could say at the time.

Adair v. *United States* involved the "yellow-dog" provision of the Erdman Act of 1898. This was a broad, regulatory law respecting railroad labor policy. Section 10 of the act specifically made illegal any labor contract part of which included a promise not to join a union upon employment. Discrimination against workers who were union members was also prohibited. The Court held section 10 of the Erdman Act unconstitutional. Speaking for the majority, Justice John M. Harlan held the provision an unreasonable interference with freedom of contract, a denial of the economic liberty protected against congressional action by the due-process clause of the Fifth Amendment. Referring particularly to the Lochner case, Harlan concluded that the statute was the kind "no government can legally justify in a free land." Holmes thought otherwise, offering his interpretation in phrases notable for clarity and candor:

> The ground on which this particular law is held bad is not so much that it deals with matters remote from commerce among the States as that it interferes with the paramount individual rights secured by the Fifth Amendment. . . . I confess that I think that the right to make contracts at will that has been derived from the word liberty in the Amendments has been stretched to its extreme by the decision. . . . Where there is, or generally is believed to be, an important ground of public policy for restraint, the Constitution does not forbid it, whether this Court agrees or disagrees with the policy pursued.

In the Adair opinion, Holmes's argument was mainly "legalistic." His dissent in the First Employers' Liability cases made use of a different approach. In 1906, Congress passed the Employers' Liability Act, which stated that every common carrier engaged in commerce in the District of Columbia or in any territory or between the states or with foreign nations was liable to its employees for damages attributable to injury or death because of the negligence of management or other employees or from material defects in tools and equipment that workers were required to use. This law, in effect, abrogated the old common law "fellow-servant" rule, under which an employer could not be held responsible for injuries that might be sustained by a worker on the job. Upon the accidental death of two railroad men soon after enactment of the statute, the railroads involved brought suit, denying the authority of the Congress to legislate for "every common carrier." The Supreme Court ruled the act bad law because no distinction was drawn between intrastate and interstate carriers. This was held to amount to an invasion of the police powers of the states appropriate to intrastate commerce. While agreeing that Congress had authority to regulate employers' liability in interstate traffic, the law as written was struck down. Holmes's willingness to depart from the majority position was arresting, inasmuch as he chose to construe the phraseology of the act loosely, perhaps because of the nature of the facts in the suit. His brief rejoinder to the Court speaks for itself:

> I must admit that I think there are strong reasons in favor of the statute adopted by a majority of the Court. But as it is possible to read words in such a way as to save the constitutionality of the Act, I think they should be taken in that narrow sense. The phrase "every common carrier engaged in trade or commerce" may be construed to mean "while engaged in trade or commerce" without violence to the habits of English speech, and to govern all that follows.

Congress acted quickly to meet the objections stated in the majority opinion, passing new legislation in 1908. In 1912, in the Second Employers' Liability cases the Supreme Court unanimously declared the new act constitutional.[31] But it was not until a major overhaul of labor law, the Norris-LaGuardia Act of 1932, that the yellow-dog contract was prohibited, by which time Holmes had left the bench.

After six years on the Supreme Court, Holmes had established a pattern of legal interpretations that lasted for the next ten. Ever the independent judge, he came down on the side of increasing federal regulations in the public interest. One example is his attitude toward a 1907 congressional law making it a punishable offense to keep alien women for purposes of prostitution within three years of entry into the country. In *Keller* v. *United States* (1909), he dissented from a majority opinion which overturned the law on the grounds that it invaded the reserve powers of the states.[32] As Holmes counterargued: "If a woman were found living in a house of prostitution within a week of her arrival, no one, I suppose, would doubt that it tended to show she was in the business when she arrived. But how far back such an inference will reach is a matter of degree, like most questions of life. And, while a period of three years may seem too long, I am not prepared to say, against the judgment of the Congress, that it is too long." Holmes was convinced that such a regulation was in the best interests of the community and should therefore be sustained by the Court. When the Mann Act of 1910, aimed at the white-slave traffic, came before the Court in *Hoke* v. *United States* (1913), he had no difficulty agreeing with the unanimous decision of the Court, written by Justice Joseph McKenna, who asserted that "the powers reserved to the states and those conferred on the nation are adapted to the exercise, whether independently or concurrently, to promote the general welfare, material and moral."[33]

Yet Holmes remained enough of his own man to fire off dissents when he found Congress or the Court exceeding their powers at the expense of the states. In *Pullman v. Kansas* (1909), the Court held as bad law a Kansas statute requiring that railroads operating within its jurisdiction pay a percentage fee levied on capitalizing.[34] Justice Harlan, speaking for the majority, decreed such a fee an unconstitutional burden on interstate commerce. Holmes thought otherwise. In an opinion in which he was joined by Chief Justice Fuller in dissent, he sought to "add a few words on the broad proposition put forward that the Constitution forbids the charge" exacted by the state. He took exception to Marshall's maxim that the power to tax is the power to destroy. Such a tax was not of necessity interference with interstate commerce if it did no more than subject that commerce to the same regulation as that imposed on local business. In another case, Holmes offered a defense of state court decisions in *Kuhn v. Fairmont Coal Company* (1909).[35] At issue was a West Virginia Supreme Court ruling which held that a coal company was not obliged to leave enough coal in the mine to support the earth above. The majority ruled that the circuit court of appeals was not bound by the state court precedent. Holmes disagreed; in his view, laws governing real estate depend on statutes and rulings of state agencies. It is not the business of the federal courts, he felt, to find arbitrary exceptions. As the facts involved conditions by nature and necessity "peculiarly local," federal interference was hardly justified. An overview of Holmes's positions in cases great and small attests to his endorsement of liberal nationalism—whatever his intention—modified by his habit of judging each case on its own merits.

By 1908, the pattern of Holmes's judicial thinking was well established; but a number of cases after that time further illustrate the play of his mind, irrespective of the concurring or dissenting character of opinions. Although Holmes voted with the majority in *Interstate Commerce Commission v. Illinois Central Railroad Company* (1910), which sustained the narrow review principle of the Hepburn Act, he joined Chief Justice White in dissenting in *Interstate Commerce Commission v. Chicago, Rock Island, and Pacific Railroad Company* (1910), siding with White against the majority because of the "idiosyncrasies of this particular case."[36] However, in the great regulating decisions of 1911—*Standard Oil Company v. United States*, *United States v. American Tobacco Company*, and *Hipolite Egg Company v. United States* (the latter case sustained the Pure Food and Drug Act)—Holmes consistently stood with the majority, endorsing regulation of corporations in the public interest.[37] But two years later, in *United States v. Winslow*, he wrote a majority opinion which refused to authorize the break-up of the United Shoe Machinery Company under the Sherman Act.[38] "On the face of it," he wrote, "the combination was simply an effort after greater efficiency." The company in question had not necessarily violated existing antitrust statutes. Consistent with the foregoing view was Holmes's dissent in *Dr. Miles Medical Company* v. *Park & Sons Company* (1911), in which he spoke of "superstitions" surrounding restraint of trade between the states.[39] "I think that, at least, it is safe to say the most enlightened judicial policy is to let people manage their own business in their own way, unless the ground for interference is very clear." Holmes argued further that, while it may be prudent to have controls on interstate traffic of necessities, he failed to see how the Dr. Miles Medical Company fit into such a category. "To let people manage their own business" had a singular Yankee ring about it. But, in fact, he was combining inherited instincts with an understanding of the law in the *Dr. Miles* case, as he also did in *Noble State Bank* v. *Haskell* (1911). Here, he cautioned "about pressing the broad words of the Fourteenth Amendment to a drily logical extreme. . . . We have few scientifically certain criteria for legislation . . . and as it often is difficult to mark the line where what is called police power by the States is limited by the Constitution of the United States, judges should be slow to read into the latter a *nolumus mutare* [we oppose change] as against the law-making power."[40]

The intensification of Progressivism from 1912 onward meant that increasing the number of cases before the Court concerned issues stemming from the wave of reform legislation. Holmes, however, continued to follow his basic judicial philosophy with little or no discernible concession to the Progressive mood. In *Cedar Rapids Gas Company* v. *Cedar Rapids* (1912), for example, he held that the utility company in question was properly regulated by an agreement that discounted the price of gas supplied to customers upon early payment of bills.[41] The company claimed that such a regulation amounted to a violation of the Fourteenth Amendment. Writing for the majority, Holmes argued that this regulation was reasonable enough. "An adjustment of this sort under a power to regulate rates has to steer between Scylla and Charybdis," he observed.

> On the one side if the franchise is taken to mean that the most profitable return that could be got, free from competition, is protected by the Fourteenth Amendment, then the power to regulate is null. On the other hand if the power to regulate withdraws the protection of the Amendment alto-

gether, then the property is nought. This is not a matter of economic theory, but a fair interpretation of a bargain.

Holmes's line of reasoning was little more than common sense applied to the law. Similarly, Holmes agreed with a majority Court stand in favor of state regulation of rail rates in the *Minnesota Rate* cases (1914), confirming the rate-making power of the Interstate Commerce Commission.[42] Holmes also believed it constitutional to institute criminal proceedings under the Sherman Act. He challenged the idea of "malice" as an essential ingredient incidental to prosecution, carrying a majority of the Court with him in *Nash* v. *United States* (1913).[43] On the other hand, in *International Harvester Company* v. *Kentucky* (1914)—and in an opinion he was at pains to insist was consistent with the *Nash* ruling—he found that the company had not violated state law when, under Kentucky statutes, producers of grain, tobacco, and other farm products raised in the state were allowed to combine in order to improve price prospects.[44] Given the facts of the case (tobacco growers had trebled their prices by means of combinations, whereas International Harvester had raised its prices by 10 to 15 percent), as well as the law itself (discrimination, at least, by implication), Holmes set down a majority opinion in favor of the plaintiff. In the sphere of trade-union activities he wrote the majority view in *Gompers* v. *United States* (1914), which justified contempt proceedings against a union leader who defied court injunctions.[45] And in *Lawlor* v. *Leowe* (1914), Holmes dissented from the majority of the Court, which exonerated the United Hatters of North America from the charge of conspiring to restrain trade in interstate commerce by recourse to a boycott.[46] "It is a tax on credulity," he said, "to ask any one to believe that members of labor unions at that time did not know that the primary and secondary boycott . . . were means expected to be employed in the effort to unionize shops." Holmes did not always follow where Progressivism might lead.

When, in 1916, Holmes was joined on the Supreme Court by Louis D. Brandeis, he was welcoming an old and trusted friend as well as a judicial mind much in sympathy with his own. At the time of his appointment, Brandeis noted that his views in regard to the Constitution were "very much those of Mr. Justice Holmes."[47] The two men had first met in 1879, when they were practicing attorneys in Boston. Not only did Brandeis gain intellectual stimulation from the friendship, but he enjoyed the society of Wendell and Fanny Holmes as well. A weekend invitation to Mattapoisett was followed by occasional dinners at the

Parker House, where the Holmeses usually dined. Brandeis was interested in what his friend had to say in his Lowell Lectures, and attended
at least one lecture during the series. He was also instrumental in per-
suading William Weld to establish the Weld Professorship at the Harvard
Law School in 1882, to which Holmes was named. When, shortly thereafter, Holmes moved to the Massachusetts bench, Brandeis wrote him:
"As one of the bar I rejoice. As part of the Law School I mourn. As your
friend I congratulate you."[48] Though their careers diverged somewhat
thereafter, the friendship remained unimpaired. Brandeis spoke pro-
phetically of "the deep impression" which Holmes would make "upon
Federal jurisprudence" on his appointment to the Supreme Court.[49] In
1909, with the case of *Muller* v. *Oregon* before the High Court—the
case in which Brandeis launched the sociological brief—Holmes was
glad enough to join the majority in upholding the state law of Oregon,
which placed restrictions on the hours women might be employed in
industry.[50] Yet, despite a definite intellectual kinship, Holmes and Brandeis had distinctly different approaches to the law. More important,
Holmes found "great comfort" in Brandeis's companionship.[51] It seemed
poetic justice laced with irony that, as Holmes was growing older in his
unintentional stand for liberalism, he was joined by the younger, more
vigorous, and deliberately liberal Brandeis. Whereas he did not always
understand the data Brandeis put forth in his opinions, in a sense a new
era had commenced on the Supreme Court, best summed up in the
soon-to-be familiar phrase, "Holmes and Brandeis dissenting."

One such dissent, typical of an almost instinctive brotherhood enjoyed by Holmes and Brandeis, came in *Southern Pacific Company* v.
Jensen (1916), a suit brought challenging a New York Workmen's Compensation law.[52] While unloading timber from a ship that had come to
New York from Galveston, a stevedore had broken his neck and died.
Under the law an award was made to the man's family, but the award
was contested on the grounds that the statute interfered with commerce
between the states and was a violation of the due process clause. Holmes
argued that it was "established" that the state had the constitutional
power to pass laws giving rights and imposing liabilities for acts done
upon the high seas, when there had been no such rights or liabilities
before. Consequently, he concluded, there was nothing to hinder the
state from so doing in the case of a maritime tort. As maritime law was
not a *corpus juris*, but "a very limited body of customs and ordinances
of the sea," the worker was justified in having some recourse at law.
"The mere silence of Congress [did not] exclude the statute or common

law of a state from supplementing the wholly inadequate maritime law of the time of the constitution in the regulation of personal rights," Holmes wrote.

Holmes and Brandeis also dissented, memorably, in *Hammer* v. *Dagenhart* (1917), with Holmes writing the opinion, joined by Justices John H. Clarke and Joseph McKenna, in what proved to be a five-to-four decision.[53] The Keating-Owen Child Labor Act of 1916 was the law at issue, a congressional statute prohibiting the shipment in interstate commerce of goods produced in factories where child labor was employed. In Holmes's opinion it was beyond dispute that the statute was within the power of the Congress to pass, that the power to regulate included the power to prohibit, that it did not matter that a supposed evil preceded or followed the transportation of goods in interstate commerce, or that the act did not meddle with anything belonging to the states. Despite the presence of Brandeis on the Court and the persistence of Holmes who was often supported by McKenna, liberal nationalism had met with a setback—the Court struck down the federal child labor law. It was actually a matter of ups and downs: The *Dagenhart* defeat pairs with *Wilson* v. *New* (1917) a case in which Holmes, Brandeis, and McKenna formed part of the majority, declaring constitutional the Adamson Eight Hour Act, limiting the hours of railway workers on interstate trains.[54]

By 1917, Oliver Wendell Holmes had been fifteen years on the Supreme Court, with another fifteen still to serve. Not yet a legend, he had won the enduring respect of his peers. Such appreciations were based, in part, on his scholar's approach to the law. Indeed, his place became known as the scholar's seat, afterwards to be occupied by Benjamin N. Cardozo and Felix Frankfurter. Holmes had displayed a penetrating knowledge of the law, erudite yet in touch with social reality. He had also developed into something of a loner on the bench, content to side with conservatives or liberals, depending on the facts of the case, the law, or the constitutional provision at issue. Such an assessment is consistent with the view of Holmes as the creator of a "new jurisprudence based on assumption which flatly contradicted some of the basic assumptions of time-honored jurisprudence." To Jerome Frank, for example, Holmes harbored revolutionary ideas which were little heeded for years but which led directly to the rise of legal realism. While there was much in the first half of his tenure on the Supreme Court to support Roscoe Pound's claim that Holmes "knew when value judgments drawn from outside of the body of authoritarian legal materials were in order," his frequent attacks on general rules and moral elements were clearly major features of his legal philosophy. Perhaps Frank's claims for Holmes as a legal realist are too exclusive; Pound insists on a moral element that is not consistently present. Such rival interpretations of Holmes's legal philosophy tend to reaffirm the image of Holmes as "his own man."[55]

Holmes was profoundly disturbed at the prospect of a world at war. When the war began in 1914, his immediate sympathies were with England—hardly surprising, given his background of study and his circle of English friends. He wrote Sir Frederick Pollock in September: "I, like the rest of us, prayed for your success against this march of Tamerlane. . . . There is no use talking about it, but my heart aches with you all." In those first days of the conflict, the enormity of the tragedy of the Great War was beyond the perceptions of most men, as patriotic people everywhere and of whatever class rallied behind their nations. Holmes, the American, tried to be detached, confessing that "in truth I should grieve only less to have German than to have English civilization broken up or hampered."[56] Even with the fighting and dying so far away, however, he found such a posture difficult. In October 1914, he told the American diplomat Lewis Einstein, "I believe in 'my country right or wrong,' and next to my country my crowd, and England is my crowd. I earnestly long to see her keep on top, and yet I shall grieve if, as I hope, Germany is crushed." And he continued: "I suppose the war was inevitable, and yet whatever the event, it fills me with sorrow, disinterested sorrow, apart from its effects upon us and from my personal sympathy with England."[57]

The American Civil War had had a shaping effect on Holmes, and, although that had been decades before, he felt a kinship with the men in the trenches. Was this vicarious experience of World War I not a reminder of how his own ordeal by fire had hardened his outlook on life? When the war spread and the United States joined the conflict in the spring of 1917, a commitment to a British triumph wedded with his own patriotic impulses. Perhaps it was partially the impact of the war, once it had become America's fight, that imparted to his judicial viewpoints thereafter their quality of judgment—as distinct from interpretation—of the law. Both the world and the nation appeared no longer able to indulge the luxury of anything less than clear-cut responses to the great issues arising from Armageddon. Doomsday—or its individual equivalent, death—seemed to stand too close to admit of ambiguous answers. Differences of opinion grew more stark in their reality, war had worked to reduce beliefs to a jarring simplicity. Judicial decisions now deserved a stand well taken, rather than theories finely spun. Or was Time finally forcing Holmes to think absolutely about Truth? Did the war, in combination with his own advancing years, at last paint him into a philosophical corner?

As useful as such consideration might be for explaining the presence of a new vein of iron in an old judge's pronouncements, part of the answer may well lie elsewhere. Had Oliver Wendell Holmes begun to believe what an increasing number of people were saying: that he was one of the wise men of the tribe and deserved to be listened to, especially in a time of crisis? Admitting that his "detachment and would-be impartiality" were "somewhat shaken" and that he would do what he could "to cherish in my countrymen an unphilosophic hatred of Germany and German ways," he was not unmindful of the veneration accorded him by many of the brightest young men in Washington during the war years.[58] And, if Truth came down to no more than things as they were, then it behooved Mr. Justice Holmes to tell it straight. Whatever the explanation, Holmes emerged over the last fifteen years of his justiceship as more the judge and, accordingly, less the legal theorist. His decisions, whether in agreement with the Court or offered in dissent, had an unmistakable cut and thrust about them.

Woodrow Wilson worried aloud about the terrible thing it would be to lead the American people into war. The kind of massive reorganization of government necessary to bring the full weight of the nation to bear on events posed new and troublesome constitutional questions, from the conscription of millions of men to the direct entrance by the federal government into economic enterprises long held to be the preserve of the business community. Under grants of power delegated him by Congress, as well as due to an accretion of authority arising from the crisis itself, President Wilson became a virtual dictator for the duration of the war. Even more disturbing was the mental and emotional conformity required of the people of the United States. Constitutional guarantees of civil and political rights were challenged, modified, and—in the thinking of many—disregarded altogether. Such were the demands of total war in the twentieth century.

The Supreme Court had no difficulty declaring the Selective Service Act constitutional in the Selective Draft Law cases (1918), nor the Army Appropriation Act which authorized presidential seizure and operation of the railroads, in *Northern Pacific Railroad Company* v. *North Dakota* (1919).[59] In each instance, the vote of the justices was unanimously in favor of the power of the sovereign state. When it came to the war and the Bill of Rights, however, the unity of the Court was eventually shattered. At issue was the constitutionality of two measures, the Espionage Act of 1917 and the Espionage Act of 1918, the latter commonly referred to as the Sedition Act. The 1917 law which guarded against efforts to disrupt the armed forces of the United States either in the process of recruitment or in military operations, came to the test in *Schenck v. United States* (1919).[60] Schenck was accused of attempting to bring about insubordination in the ranks of the armed forces by causing to have mailed to individuals who had been called up under the draft a document designed to incite disobedience to the law. He was charged further with using the mails to transmit his plea, sending material the law declared unmailable. As general secretary of the Socialist party, Schenck personally supervised the printing and distribution of 15,000 pieces of mail to inductees. The gist of his defense was that the Selective Service Act contravened the first section of the Thirteenth Amendment, which protected against involuntary servitude. Holmes delivered the unanimous judgment of the Court, which found Schenck guilty and the Selective Service law constitutional. The essence of his argument can be reduced to a few sentences.

> We admit that in many places and in ordinary times the defendants in saying all that was said in the circular would have been within their constitutional rights. But the character of every act depends upon circumstances in which it is done. . . . The most stringent protection of free speech would not protect a man in falsely shouting fire in a theater and causing a panic. It does not even protect a man from an injunction against uttering words that may have all the effect of force. . . . The question in every case is whether the words used are used in such circumstances and are of such a nature as to create a clear and present danger that they will bring about the substantive evils that Congress has a right to prevent. It is a question of proximity and degree.
>
> When a nation is at war many things that might be said in time of peace are such a hindrance to its effort that their utterance will not be endured so long as men fight and then no court would regard them as protected by any constitutional right. It seems admitted that if an actual obstruction of the recruiting of service were proved, liability for words that produced that effect might be enforced.

The "clear and present danger" rule which Holmes had enunciated, and by which the *Schenck* case became distinguished, was akin to the "rule of proximate causation" found in the common law both of England

and America. The finality of Holmes's judgment in the case is better appreciated from his remarks to Harold Laski, written the day the *Schenck* decision was handed down. "[The] real substance [of the case] being: "Damn your eyes—that's the way it's going to be."[61] In wars, Holmes was saying, there are only friends and enemies, the finer shadings of the law being lost temporarily in the blinding flash of passions. Holmes wrote two other majority opinions at this time which tend to show that the power of the sovereign state, when confronted by the rights of its citizens, must prevail. A certain Frohwerk appealed to the Supreme Court to reverse a lower court decision that declared him guilty of violating the Espionage Act of 1917 by reason of his publication of a newspaper, the *Missouri Staats Zeitung*.[62] His appeal was based especially on the guarantees provided him by the First Amendment. In reply for the Court, Holmes answered, in part:

> to that argument we think it necessary to add what has been said in *Schenck v. United States*, only that the First Amendment, while prohibiting legislation against free speech as such, can not have been, and obviously was not, intended to give immunity for every possible use of language. . . . We venture to believe that neither Hamilton nor Madison, nor any other competent person then or later, ever supposed that to make criminal the counseling of a murder within the jurisdiction of Congress would be unconstitutional interference with free speech.

The motivation of Frohwerk in seeking to discourage the American war effort was nationalistic—his newspaper spoke of the "unconquerable spirit and the undiminished strength of the German nation"—but motivations were irrelevant to the operation of the law and thus to the judgments set down by Holmes. The other case, consistent with the *Schenck* and *Frohwerk* judgments, was that of *Debs v. United States* (1919).[63] The protests of Debs against the war were based on a mixture of socialism and pacifism. Holmes's majority opinion simply cited the *Schenck* case and its reasoning. As he confided to Laski, "in the only question before us I could not doubt about the law." At the same time, he admitted that he "greatly regretted having to write" the *Debs* ruling, expressing doubts about the wisdom of the government in pressing either the Frohwerk or the Debs indictments: "Of course I know that donkeys and knaves would represent us as concurring in the condemnation of Debs because he was a dangerous agitator. Of course too, as far as that is concerned, he [Debs] might split his guts without my interfering with him or sanctioning interference."[64] Such private thoughts, though intimating a possible alteration of views on the issue of constitutional guarantees under the First Amendment, were insufficient to persuade Holmes to abandon the letter of the law.

But he was about to alter his judgment. The Sedition Act of 1918 provided for far more sweeping restrictions on freedom of speech than had the earlier law, under which all the foregoing cases had been argued. So extreme were these limitations on free speech that Holmes and Brandeis were quick to utter doubts about its application. The key was *Abrams v. United States* (1919).[65] In the long view, it proved also to be a pivotal case in Holmes's thinking about First Amendment guarantees. Throughout the 1920s, in a series of suits, Holmes and Brandeis dissented from the majority, registering their belief in individual freedoms, the initial expression of which came in the *Abrams* case.

Abrams and his cohorts had printed and scattered from rooftops a few thousand leaflets protesting the dispatch of American troops to Russia at the time of the Bolshevik revolution. A majority of the Court chose to uphold a lower court conviction of the individuals in question, whereupon Abrams appealed to the Supreme Court for a reversal of judgment on the grounds that his First Amendment freedoms had been denied. The Court, speaking through Justice Clarke, deemed the evidence ample that Abrams had sought to obstruct the American war effort in a manner that violated the Espionage (Sedition) Act of 1918. The rule applied was that of "bad tendency," a less stringent test than "clear and present danger" and thus a stricter limitation of freedom of expression. Holmes demurred. Having given the Court's ruling in the *Schenck, Frohwerk,* and *Debs* cases, "I thought it proper to state what I thought the limits of the doctrine," as he explained to Pollock.[66] He objected in the first place to the evidence, declaring the message of the leaflets too vague and in fact too silly to be a distraction from the war effort. It was not enough that the actions of the accused had created a "bad tendency." Proof was needed that the leaflets had created a "clear and present danger" since the punishment meted out, twenty years in prison, spoke the dimension of the crime. And yet there was much more to Holmes's dissent than reservations about the evidence. He noted his belief the defendant had as much right to publish what he had, as the government had to publish the Constitution "now vainly invoked" by him. Holmes then gave voice to the central proposition of what may be termed a liberal rendering of the Bill of Rights:

> Persecution for the expression of opinions seems to me perfectly logical. If you have no doubt of your premises or your power and want a certain

result with all your heart you naturally express your wishes in law and sweep away all opposition. To allow opposition by speech seems to indicate that you think the speech impotent, as when a man says that he has squared the circle, or that you do not care wholeheartedly for the result, or that you doubt either your power or your premises. But when men have realized that time has upset many fighting faiths, they may come to believe even more than they believe the very foundations of their conduct that the ultimate good desired is better reached by free trade in ideas-that the best test of truth is the power of the thought to get itself accepted in the competition of the market; and that truth is the only ground upon which their wishes can be carried out. That, at any rate, is the theory of our Constitution. It is an experiment, as all life is an experiment. Every year, if not every day, we have to wager our salvation upon some prophecy based upon imperfect knowledge. While that experiment is part of our system I think that we should be eternally vigilant against attempts to check the expression of opinions that we loathe and believe to be fraught with death, unless they so imminently threaten immediate interference with the lawful and pressing purpose of the law that an immediate check is required to save the country.[67]

Such is the stuff of which judgments are made. Nor is the impact of this eloquent statement weakened by Holmes's private remark that he took "the extremist view in favor of free speech (in which, in the abstract, I have no very enthusiastic belief, though I hope I would die for it)."[68] To note that Holmes had become more judgmental and less interpretative underscores the paradoxes of his thought: his confessed lack of enthusiasm, be it remembered, was for an abstraction; but his hope of dying in defense of free speech, were it to come about, would be a hard fact. Holmes believed, above all, in hard facts: that which "he could not help but believe" was, for him, true. In this subtle yet obvious way, he came to grips with the right of free speech and other personal liberties, and in the last dozen years or so of his justiceship judged cases accordingly.

Contrasts between the busy life of William Howard Taft over the first twenty years of the new century and the sequestered days of Oliver Wendell Holmes serving as an associate justice come sharply to mind. Yet appearances may be deceiving. All the while, Taft harbored thoughts that one day he would attain a seat on the High Court, and perhaps the chief justiceship might one day be his. As for Holmes, never for a moment did he view himself as being hors de combat because he was an associate justice. On the contrary, the Court was, for him, the judicial equivalent of the battlefield. To have continued as a law school professor was his idea of being out of the line of fire. To be a judge in Massachusetts and a fortiori, to be a justice of the Supreme Court was to be in action. The proceedings before the High Court were replete with drama and danger, as decisions affecting the entire nation were arrived at. It was a place where the tough-minded—of which he was one—could thrive and triumph.

What was to distinguish William Howard Taft's conduct of court affairs was a determination to mold a "Taft court," that is, one reflecting his own understanding of the Constitution. He had taken the work of John Marshall as his model. Holmes, on the other hand, came to believe in himself as a master of his craft, able to draw on nearly forty years of judging, twenty of which dealt directly with constitutional issues, and in the course of which he had won honor and admiration. During the tenures of Chief Justices Fuller and White, Holmes had come into his own. There was no reason to believe he would not hold his own under Taft, however much their understanding and application of the law might differ. They each believed that it was a living law they must interpret in the best interests of the nation.

4
The 1920s Court

WILLIAM HOWARD TAFT WAS NOMINATED CHIEF JUSTICE OF THE UNITED States on June 30, 1921; the Senate confirmed the President's choice the same day, with only four dissenting votes. After years of waiting, the frustrations he had lived with were suddenly dissolved. That place in public service was now his which he believed he should have, by right of legal philosophy and ambition. The fact is, in 1921, Taft insisted that any appointment to the bench be that of chief justice. Had he accepted earlier offers to name him, he would have been content as an associate justice. But, after the presidency, nothing less than to become the high priest of the "sacred shrine," as he once referred to the Court, would suffice. Such an attitude was not, however, based on pride of place. Taft had long been a critical, if friendly, observer of the operation of the High Court and of the entire federal judiciary. He, better than most, realized that it was a system that badly needed reorganization and leadership, that it required the hand of an experienced executive. Without the application of drastic reform measures, he feared that the Court, by falling further and further behind in its work-it might take up to two years for a case to be heard once it was entered on the Supreme Court docket-could simply become irrelevant. A dangerous prospect at any time, but the more so when the onslaught of Progressive legislation required the scrutiny of nine wise jurists. Only as chief justice could Taft have the opportunity to revitalize the operations of the court.[1]

Good fortune is sometimes the unintended result of good tactics. Taft could not have suspected the crucial contribution Warren Harding was to make in his quest for the chief justiceship; but the fact remains that he greatly favored Harding's effort to win the Ohio statehouse in 1910. He discerned in the future President a man "attractive in many ways," and contributed $5,000 to the Republican campaign in Ohio that year. Although Harding did not win the governorship, he was elected to the Senate in 1914. Meanwhile, Elihu Root had chosen Harding to place

Taft's name in nomination at the 1912 Republican convention, with Taft's hearty approval. He predicted that Harding had a "great future." In playing the political game, Taft was taking the position that had gained him party favor as a young man in the 1880s: close to the seats of the mighty to profit from their favor, but distant enough to remain uncorrupted. Taft actively supported Harding's candidacy in 1920. As a Republican ex-President, he proclaimed himself ready to help the new President meet the demands of office.

In late December, Taft made the prescribed trip to Marion, Ohio, to visit the President-elect. People who knew Harding well were not surprised at what took place, though Taft himself was temporarily thrown off stride. After a pleasant breakfast, the two men retired to the parlor to discuss political affairs. Without warning, Harding interjected: "By the way. I want to ask you, would you accept a position on the Supreme Bench because if you would, I'll put you on the court." According to his own account. Taft responded at some length, his most salient point being that he could accept no appointment save that of chief justice. Harding remained noncommittal, and the talks ended. Eager to exploit the opening provided him, the next day Taft wrote Harding to thank him. In the letter he went on to say that Chief Justice White had often voiced his preference for Taft as a successor. He could not have made his position more plain.

White was in poor health; in truth, he was a dying man. The end came in May 1921, but Harding failed to act promptly to fill the chief justiceship. He had also made certain promises to George Sutherland of Utah regarding a Court position, and, as the Court was not sitting at the time, there was no pressing need to act. Taft did not propose to stand still, however. He enlisted the support of such powerful Republicans as Senator Lodge, and of administration officials, including Attorney General Harry Daugherty. As a spokesman for the administration, Daugherty had gone on record as favoring Court reform to relieve the logjam of cases; and he, in turn, urged the President to avoid any delay in naming Taft as chief justice. Harding relented, and the announcement came at the end of June. William Howard Taft's plate remained right side up. At age sixty-four, the most exciting and productive part of his career lay just ahead. The safest of harbors had been reached at last.[2]

The Taft Court, 1921–1930, revealed the influence of the Chief Justice in a variety of ways. Under his direction was carried out the most thorough reform of the Court system since Oliver Ellsworth had drafted the Judiciary Act of 1789. In order to persuade Congress to pass the

Judges Act of 1922 and the Judges Act of 1925, the Chief Justice became an activist, lobbying on Capitol Hill and before such interested parties as the American Bar Association—all to good effect. As a former President and a Republican, he felt at ease offering advice—sometimes solicited, sometimes gratuitous—which was sometimes taken by Presidents Harding, Coolidge, and Hoover. Although he had been a poor politician in elective politics, he was quite successful in playing the game as a jurist. He took pains to control the choice of federal judges, from the district courts far and wide to the High Court in Washington. Operating on the premise that the office of chief justice might be as big and as active as the person who occupied it—a premise he had put forth about the Presidency in 1906—when it came to deciding cases, Taft used his considerable charm, skill, and willingness to compromise to "mass the Court." He participated fully in the processes of adjudication and writing opinions. From 1921 to 1930, Taft wrote 253 of the 1,596 opinions delivered. Looked at another way, he averaged thirty opinions a term, to his colleagues' twenty. He was not simply the high priest but a workhorse of his own Court.

Taft dominated the Court for a decade. Given the strong personalities of Justices Holmes and Brandeis and their legal philosophies, which were often at odds with Taft's, this is a remarkable assertion. It suggests that Taft had all along been correct in his self-assessment: the highest court in the land was his natural milieu. As for the chief justiceship, his effectiveness in that position was the result of wide experience as an administrator in Manila and Washington. This merely underscores an irony of Taft's career. Without the administrative experience that came about because he had reluctantly walked a political path after 1900, his achievements as chief justice could have been considerably less impressive. It was the combination of legal knowledge, judicial temperament, and administrative know-how that gave the Taft Court a distinctive dimension. Nellie Taft, to compound the irony, had a vital, if unintentional, part in making William Howard Taft a successful chief justice. She had insisted that her husband forsake his first federal judgeship for such rewards and training as politics had to offer.

William Howard Taft's first purpose was to streamline the federal judiciary, from the district level to the Supreme Court.[3] It was a system much in need of renovation. Congress had never used its power to construct a unified, well-coordinated system of courts. District courts had become virtually self-contained and were a rule unto themselves with regard to the handling of cases. Certain districts were overloaded

with work, while others dealt with few cases. But there was no authority
vested in the chief justice or any other officer to direct an equitable
distribution of the case load to achieve a speedier disposition of cases
and, not incidentally, a speedier dispensation of justice. The chief justice
was, at best, the nominal head of the national courts system. The situation at the Supreme Court was further complicated because the Court
could exercise little discretion in the cases that came before it: a case
of no great constitutional consequence vied with one of significance,
and both cases had to be heard in turn. The delays involved were not
only exasperating; they were negative in effect because they tended to
reflect a poor image of dispensing justice.

Taft's concern for improving the operation of the entire judiciary went
back to his circuit court days. Because he had served as dean of the
Cincinnati Law School at the time, his experience as a sitting judge
and as a law school administrator and professor made the faults of the
system particularly glaring to him. Despite a nonjudicial career after
1900, Taft continued to study the courts in operation. In June 1908, he
wrote "The Law of the Country" for the *North American Review,* which
amounted to a point-by-point critique of the judicial system. Taft argued
that "our failure to secure expedition and thoroughness in the enforcement of public and private rights in our Courts was the case in which
we had fallen farthest short of the ideal conditions in the whole of our
Government." Taft accounted it worse than the "defects in our system
of municipal government which are notorious." In particular he identified the number of allowable appeals, overelaborate codes of procedure,
expense of litigation, and dilatory judges among the chief evils calling
for reform.

Once he became president, Taft had pressed for action in these and
other areas. In his annual messages to Congress he dwelt on the situation. "In my judgment a change of judicial procedure, with a view to
reducing its expense to private litigants in civil cases and facilitating the
dispatch of business and final decisions in both civil and criminal cases,
constitutes the greatest need in our American institutions," he announced in his first annual message.[4] On another occasion he urged
Congress to confine the jurisdiction of the Supreme Court "almost
wholly to statutory and constitutional questions," and asked the legislature to appoint a committee to investigate the entire federal court system
to determine what measures of reform should be pursued. While president, Taft took care that only well-qualified men entered the federal
judiciary. "The party leaders may name the political office holders, but

as long as I am President, no man shall ascend [the federal bench] except for reason of qualification for that high and sacred office, regardless of politics."[5]

By 1914, Taft had clarified his ideas for modernizing the courts. In "Attacks on the Courts and Legal Procedures" he proposed that power be conferred "upon the head of the Federal judicial system, either the Chief Justice or a council of judges appointed by him, or by the Supreme Court, to consider each year the pending judicial business of the country and to distribute the Federal judicial force of the country through the various district courts and intermediate appeals courts."[6] Taft was to modify this proposal at a later time; but, once he was chief justice, he sought to have the basic idea of his 1914 statement enacted into law.

The inherent deficiencies Taft deplored were worsened by the great mass of litigation growing out of World War I and the passing of the Eighteenth Amendment. Both civil and criminal cases involving espionage, civil liberties, wartime business contracts, and like cases crowded court dockets, while the government's efforts to enforce national prohibition added to a growing backlog. Litigation arising from prohibition alone accounted for an eight percent rise in the number of cases. Only Congress had the authority to revise court procedures, provide for more judges, and impart badly needed flexibility to the system. Without leadership from the judiciary, however, to explain fully the growing desperation of the courts' situation, little was going to be done. Chief Justice White had no stomach for this line of action, which he thought might break down the separation of the political branches of government from the judiciary. Taft, in contrast, was eager to take up the fight. It was a formidable task, certain to invoke legislative suspicions and lead to opposition; but Taft embraced leadership as his primary responsibility upon becoming chief justice.

He had been in office only two months when he opened his campaign for reform. Addressing the American Bar Association in Cincinnati in August 1921, the Chief Justice complained of the congestion in the district courts. Because of the "general enlargement of the jurisdiction of the courts under the enactment by Congress of laws which are the exercise of its heretofore dormant powers" "something must be done to give to the federal courts a judicial force that can grapple these arrears and end them."[7] Speaking before the ABA in Chicago, four months later, Taft proposed three major reforms: "first, an increase in the judicial force in the trial federal courts and an organization and effective distribution of the force by a council of judges; second, simplicity of procedure in the trial federal courts; and third, a reduction in the obligatory jurisdiction of the Supreme Court and an increase in the field of its discretionary jurisdiction by certiorari."[8] The proposal that a council of judges organize and administer the federal courts was immediately controversial.

Taft's particularization of the council-of-judges idea (that is, administrative power to be exercised by the chief justice and the nine senior circuit judges), upon conference with the attorney general, was cast in statutory form by Attorney General Daugherty. Taft had a look at the draft and, after making one or two technical adjustments, approved the proposal. The bill was submitted to the Senate and referred to the Judiciary Committee. Actively seeking passage of the bill, the Chief Justice testified before this committee on two occasions, telling the senators: "the principle of this bill is the executive principle of having some head to apply judicial force at the strategic points where the arrears have so increased that it needs a mass of judges to get rid of them."[9] In following up this general comment, Taft made any number of criticisms, which he addressed specifically before the Judiciary Committee: that there was much stuffing of dockets, so that many cases could be readily dismissed; that judges and their clerks could discern an important constitutional issue in a case; that district judges "not infrequently" grew indifferent to their responsibilities because they were answerable to no one. In essence, Taft was appealing for efficiency based on responsibility, very much in the Progressive mode and a useful reminder that instrumentalism in government may be appropriated by conservatives to help achieve their purposes.

The Chief Justice was both angered and scandalized by some of the senatorial objections to the judicial conference, since many of the criticisms seemed to trivialize the whole concept. Senator Shields of Tennessee described it "as a great social function of the Judiciary of the United States, presided over by the Chief Justice in Washington or some other nice place. All expenses are to be paid or at least $10 a day and traveling expenses are allowed. Let any Senator examine this provision, and if he can really find any merit except that of a social function, I shall be astonished."[10] Senator Walsh of Montana dismissed the judicial conference in much the same fashion: "It means absolutely nothing on earth except a junket and a dinner."[11]

But opposition to the bill was deadly serious as well. On the whole, Congress was dubious about the wisdom of authorizing the conference to assign judges. Senator Shields argued that it was "not a judicial power and does not in the remotest manner concern the exercise of the jurisdiction of the Supreme Court. The judicial power is the power to try and determine controversies . . . the power to establish courts and provide them with judges is a legislative power, Congress alone has this power."[12]

Because Taft had been so forthright and forceful in expressing his views to the Senate Judiciary Committee, he had put the passage of the bill at some risk. Senator Shields charged that the Anti-Saloon League (it was well-known that the Chief favored prohibition) was backing the bill because it would give the chief justice the power to assign more and more judges to try cases involving violations of the Volstead Act. Beyond that, any kind of special interest might seek to influence the selection of judges, with justice ill served as a result. Some senators questioned the propriety of the Chief Justice coming before the Judiciary Committee at all, on the grounds that such action violated the separation-of-powers principle and was therefore possibly unconstitutional. Others contended that the presence of the attorney general at the judicial conference marked explicit rejection of the separation-of-powers rule.

The considerable opposition the bill faced required the submission of an alternate proposal in 1922. Soon Congressmen had come round to supporting the fundamental proposition that the courts as then organized were unequal to their constitutionally assigned tasks. Representative Joseph Walsh of Massachusetts agreed that a conference could accomplish a good deal more than "letters written from all over the country. . . . A Conference would result in uniformity and tend toward the dispatch of business."[13] Senator Cummins of Iowa, a force to be reckoned with in the Senate, was more positive:

> Instead of having disjointed and disconnected communications between the Chief Justice and the various circuit judges, we have provided for a meeting at which the requirements of all the districts can be considered and compared, and if it is necessary to designate judges for work outside their districts, it can be done with some comprehension of the real needs of the country, and it can be done in no other way.[14]

The Chief Justice could not have said it better.

The obvious need for judicial reform, Taft's persistence. and the support of the American Bar Association crystallized Congressional endorsement. The Judges Act passed the Senate by a vote of 36 to 16 and the House by 139 to 78, and it was signed into law in September 1922. Admittedly, Taft did not get all he wanted in the legislation as it was finally written, but the power was now in the hands of the chief justice to relieve crowded dockets, while the judicial conference clothed him with an undeniable executive character. The national judiciary was now more self-directed.

In spite of the dire predictions of judicial usurpation, the conferences under Taft's direction were matter-of-fact affairs. The Chief presided; reports were submitted by the attorney general with regard to the amount of business facing each court, along with an assessment of state dockets. The attorney general also made known to the conference complaints against judges which his office had received, and offered recommendations for improving court operations. The 1922 and 1923 conferences took up the matter of proposed legislation, which was enacted in 1925, respecting the reduction in the number of cases to come before the Supreme Court on writ of certiorari. The first conference also established committees to make recommendations regarding the transfer of judges, rules of procedure, dead litigation, and similar technical matters. On occasion, the Chief Justice made use of the conference in ways not specifically provided for in the statute. He was concerned, for example, with uniform sentences for prohibition violators, called for improved libraries for district judges, and sought to lay down guidelines to expedite the handling of cases. Taft became the first chief justice to lead the federal judiciary in a meaningful way. Not that the conferences amounted to a grab for power. As always, Taft was careful of the Constitution and continued to hold that the meetings of judges should be confined largely to "an examination of a judge's capacity to dispose of his caseload." Only when this new state of affairs is compared with the total lack of such authority on the part of his immediate predecessors, Chief Justices Fuller and White, does the power of Chief Justice Taft stand out. Passage of the Judges Act of 1922 amounted to a "great victory," with other challenges lying directly ahead.

The second objective in Taft's overall plans for judicial reform was the limitation of cases heard on appeal by the Supreme Court. He aimed to give the Court the authority to allow only cases of constitutional importance to come before it by certifying them on writ. Even before passage of the 1922 Act, Taft had begun to stress the burdens under which the High Court was laboring. "The situation is rendered critical," he told an ABA gathering in the summer of 1922, "by the accumulating mass of litigation growing out of the war, and especially claims against the government which, if allowed to come under the present law to the Supreme Court, will throw us hopelessly behind schedule.[15] "As his

profile had been highly visible in the fight for the 1922 statute, Taft
appointed a committee of associate justices to help draft this legislation,
to be known as the Judges Act of 1925. He did so at the behest of
Senator Cummins, chairman of the Judiciary Committee. Despite this
maneuver, the familiar opponents of reform had their say. Senator Walsh
insisted that the bill was another power grab. It was a truism, he said,
that "a good court always seeks to extend its jurisdiction," and that "the
appetite for power grows as it is gratified."[16] Even former Associate Justice Hughes was heard to express some reservations about the proposed
changes. Such doubts combined with the need of Congress to attend to
more pressing legislative matters to delay passage of the second Judges
Act until February 1925. The significant Senate vote was seventy-six to
one. It was a second major victory for reform, and as the Chief Justice
had had a part in formulating the proposal for consideration by the
Judiciary Committee-though his role was somewhat clandestine-he must
share the credit.

For the remainder of his tenure, Taft looked to the enactment of
additional measures to complete the modernizing process. Ideally this
would have included a thorough revision of the Judicial Code, but for
that there was little real prospect. His more modest suggestion of
allowing the Supreme Court—in pursuance of specific legislative
grants—to simplify rules of procedure for federal courts received insufficient support, for that matter. The limits of judicial reform had been
reached. Notwithstanding, Taft's contribution to the administration of
the law, both substantively and in terms of executive leadership, had
been impressive, earning him a unique place in the history of the federal judiciary.

Chief Justice Taft displayed an unusual flair in an office historically
looked upon as a place remote from both politics and society. This came
about because of his zest for judging, which was carried to ultimate
heights as head of the Supreme Court. As he once remarked, the chief
justiceship is "comfort, dignity, and power without worry."[17] He was
happy in his work because it suited him, and he was eager to share his
enthusiasm with those around him. Down to 1927, at least, Taft was a
singularly successful chief justice. "Things go happily in the conference
room with Taft," Justice Brandeis reported: "the judges go home less
tired emotionally and less weary physically than in White's day."[18] Taft
made it a point to encourage his colleagues, and especially the narrow-
minded Justice James C. McReynolds, to adopt a tolerant attitude toward
Brandeis, the first Jewish member of the Supreme Court. The maladroit

President had become the persuasive jurist. Only in his last year in office, which was the last year of his life, did Taft slacken his pace. After 1926, the Court was sharply divided in its constitutional philosophy, and its decisions were based on divergent assessments of the law.

As Taft filled up his days and nights with the extrajudicial business of the Court, Holmes continued to reflect on legal ultimates. His theory of law, its origins and its essence, received an unambiguous, if somewhat negative, statement in his essay, "Natural Law," which appeared in 1918.[19] In it, Holmes again directly challenged those who continued to hold the law as an absolute, having its source in God or the state or the inalienable rights of man. Decrying man's tendency to demand the superlative, which he thought well illustrated in the "jurist's search for criteria of universal validity," Holmes invoked the standard of force. Truth "was the majority vote of that nation which can lick all others." Putting the same basic idea more adroitly, he spoke of truth as "the system of my intellectual limitations," that is, what he and the majority of his fellow human beings could not help but believe. Admitting that deep seated prejudices can not be argued about Holmes noted that different men adhere to different prejudices; and, he continued, if these "prejudices are sufficiently far reaching we try to kill the other man rather than let him have his way." Truth—in some fixed form, in other words, whether in life or in the law did not exist, and judges who sought it or claimed to have found it—he dismissed as naive. Holmes fortified his position by arguing that he did "not see any rational ground for demanding the superlative-for being dissatisfied unless we are assured that our truth is cosmic truth . . . that the ultimates of a little creature on this little earth are the last word of the unimaginable whole." Instead, he concluded, "it is enough for us that the universe has produced us and has within it, as less than it, all that we believe and love." "Natural Law," blunt in its message, was a powerful essay, despite negative inflections. Holmes was once again the acknowledged spokesman of a philosophy of legal realism which had cut itself loose from the old moral moorings. Critics of legal realism complained that Holmes and the like-minded were adrift. Holmes saw it another way. "Philosophy does not furnish motives," he wrote in "Natural Law," "but it shows men that they are not fools for doing what they already want to do." For scientific man in the twentieth century, principle followed action rather than action following principle. This was a general rule of life to which the law was no exception. "Natural Law" was to be the last major public statement Holmes was to offer, apart from his Court opinions. As such it was "pure" Holmes.

The fact is, Holmes was less and less inclined to write the formal article. As he grew older—and in 1921, when Taft assumed the chief justiceship, Holmes was in his eighty-first year—he was content to express himself, off the record, to two devoted friends and correspondents, Frederick Pollock and Harold Laski. Their correspondence over the 1920s reveals a truer Holmes. Take, for example, Holmes's estimate of Taft as shared with Laski at the time Taft's appointment to the chief justiceship was pending. "Taft is much mentioned. I would rather have Hughes. . . . Hughes is a hard worker. Taft is said to be indolent. He has beeen out of judicial place for 20 years or so—and though he did well as a circuit judge, I never saw anything that struck me as more than first rate second rate. I have heard it said and denied that he is hard to get along with if you don't agree with him."[20] Once Taft had been named to the post, Holmes reiterated his reservations, repeating the first-rate, second-rate evaluation, and adding: "but this is strictly private and I may be wrong."[21] In writing on the same matter to Pollock, Holmes was more circumspect, but then Laski had the knack of typically drawing out the most acerbic comments from him. To Pollock: "I am looking forward with curiosity to the new Chief Justice. He marked a fundamental difference in our way of thinking by saying this office always had been his ambition. The only thing I feel is to believe when the end comes . . . that one has touched the superlative. . . . Between ourselves I doubt Mr. Taft can do that."[22] Clearly, Holmes was dubious about Harding's nominee.

Once Taft took up the reins, Holmes was open and fair-minded. With the start of the 1921 term, he told Pollock: "I think the new Chief Justice promises well." In "his way of disposing of executive details, Taft seems likely to take them easily and get through them without friction. In Mass. and here I have seen the difference that this makes in the wear and tear incident to critical meetings."[23] By the following year, Holmes had summed up his response to Taft by informing Pollock that "we are very happy with the present Chief. . . . He is good humored, laughs readily, not quite rapid enough, but does keep things moving." Further, he noted that some of Taft's written opinions were on "a pretty high level" and that "the other day he expressed the movement of interstate commerce in a large and rather masterly way."[24] Coming from Holmes, this was no small praise. His respect for Taft was, in fact, sustained; as late as September 1927, anticipating the start of another Court term, he wrote Pollock: "It is very pleasant with the present Chief."[25] To Laski, however, he could be more critical, complaining that Taft had not taken his advice about urging their fellow justices "to return their opinions more promptly."[26] But such were Taft's skills as a judicial administrator and jurist that Holmes expressed admiration to Laski, praising his opinion in *Stafford* v. *Wallace*, saying that "it gave him great satisfaction."[27] And he consistently complimented the Chief for the smooth way in which he conducted the everyday business of the Court. Throughout the 1920s, Holmes recognized the former President as "the chief," and as *his* chief, giving added meaning to the term "Taft court."

Letters by Holmes to Pollock and Laski written just after World War I and on into the Taft era yield a number of insights into Holmes's thinking about the law and his way of interpreting it. Indeed, there is a stronger sense of the judgmental as the aging justice moved into the 1920s. He was supremely confident of his ruling in the Debs case and complained of receiving letters from people who were disturbed because they believed Debs had been unfairly found guilty under a law which itself was suspect. Holmes insisted that, as far as the law and the Espionage Act of 1918 were concerned, "there was no doubt that the Jury was warranted in finding him guilty or that the law was Constitutional."[28] This was a position from which he did not budge.

As early as 1919, the often to be invoked phrase, "Holmes and Brandeis dissenting" had come into vogue. The new justice had a capacious mind that the old justice readily respected. "Brandeis the other day drove a harpoon into my midriff with reference to my summer occupation," he confided to Pollock. "He said you talk about improving your mind, you only exercise it on subjects with which you are familiar. Why don't you study something new, study some domain of fact. Take up the textile industries in Mass. and after reading the reports sufficiently you can go to Lawrence and get a human notion of how it really is." Holmes continued his account of the talking-to Brandeis had administered with this protest: "I hate facts. I always say the chief end of man is to form general propositions—adding that no general proposition is worth a damn. Of course a general proposition is simply a string for the facts and I have little doubt that it would be good for my immortal soul to plunge into them, good also for the performance of my duties but I shrink from the bore."[29] Judgments, it seems, were for Holmes, more easily made without the facts. Having been "harpooned," he confessed to Laski that he was impressed by Brandeis's suggestion, "supposing it would be good for him to get into the actualities touching spindles—immigration—God knows what, but I would rather meditate on the initial push and following spin."[30]

As may be imagined, Holmes's letters were often replete with worthy gossip, with Pollock in particular, probably because of the relative ages of the two men and his respect for Sir Frederick's legal erudition. Holmes was proud of his majority opinion in the Arizona Employers' Liability case, even if some of his fellow justices found his arguments overdrawn. In ruling that "all the risks of the employees be thrown on the employers," he was one with the Progressives, by this date a dying breed.[31] He was also especially keen to explain again his position in the Abrams case about which he appeared to be defensive in writing both his friends. Specifically, he held that the government had failed to prove that Abrams and his leaflets were intended to hinder the war effort. Holmes's resort to Abrams's "intention" appears as another example of the increasingly judgmental quality of his outlook, even though it was cast in negative terms.[32] On another occasion, when discussing a series of complex cases, cases for which he had been assigned to write majority opinions, he thought to quote Dr. Johnson: "be rid of your mind of scruples," advice Holmes appeared willing to take himself.

The gossip sometimes turned serious, as it did when Holmes had news of the death of James Bryce in January 1922. "Thus breaks one of the oldest associations that I had with living men," he confessed to Pollock "We intimately mixed rather than chemically bonded, but the mixture was so intimate that the loss is great to me as, no doubt, to you."[33] Holmes and Bryce had spent two days together at Beverley Farms the previous summer; he recalled to Laski his impressions, which, in light of the foregoing words to Pollock, are noteworthy. To Laski: "found Bryce very alert and well rounded, but he has outlived his superlatives, I should think, which I think is a loss." Ever the skeptic when writing to Laski, Holmes added: "Perhaps I should say, I doubt if he ever had them."[34] Such a mordant comment may have reflected Holmes's larger concern about his own advancing years. In an earlier letter to Pollock, he admitted with playful seriousness: "I take a little more pleasure in 'Elegy in a Country Church Yard' and a little less in Browning."[35] The question left unanswered is: How would Holmes's mindset address the new and perplexing issues sure to emerge over the years of the Taft Court, as well as other basic points of law which have a way of surfacing irrespective of the times and the customs? To put the question another way, How would Taft respond to Holmes and the thinking of the other justices, from Joseph McKenna, an 1898 McKinley appointee, to Harlan Fiske Stone, named by Coolidge in 1925?

Of the two justices who tended to be court mavericks, Taft was more likely to respect the reasoning of Holmes than Brandeis. By 1921, Holmes was well on his way to becoming a legend. Past eighty when Taft took charge of the Court, Holmes had not so much altered his legal outlook as he had softened its expression; although he was still ready to deliver a sardonic thrust if the opportunity presented itself. The Chief felt a certain kinship with Holmes because he was a New Englander, a feeling traceable perhaps to the Emersonian idealism Holmes had imbibed in his youth, as had Taft's father, who passed it on to his son. Speaking of Holmes, the Chief Justice deemed it a "great comfort to have such a well of pure common law undefiled immediately next to one so that one can drink and be sure of getting the pure article."[36] Although he often disagreed with the Chief's interpretation of the Constitution and the law, Holmes had the utmost respect for Taft. At first the venerable justice found Taft a great tonic after the less-than-dynamic White. He liked Taft's friendly manner, his easy laughter, and his determination to "keep things moving pleasantly."[37] As the years passed, however, while there was no falling out, a cooling was perceptible in their relationship. Taft complained of Holmes's dissents, to which the Justice responded that he had no choice but to dissent from bad legal opinions. Taft came to believe that Holmes's reading of the Constitution was flawed by a questionable ethical relativity and that he lacked experience in affairs of government, which would have kept him sound on the Constitution. Furthermore, was not Holmes getting too old; and, if not that, was he not under the sway of Justice Brandeis to the degree that Brandeis usually had two votes in a case, his own and that of O. W. Holmes, Jr.? Despite such strains, Taft never lost his affection for his colleague. When Fanny Holmes, the Justice's wife of more than fifty years, died, it was the Chief Justice who stepped in to relieve his grieving partner of the cares of arranging for funeral and burial. Taft had a plot at Arlington set aside where Holmes himself would be laid to rest amid his old comrades of the 20th Massachusetts Infantry. Holmes was deeply touched. He wrote to Laski: "How can one help loving a man with such a kind heart." Ever considerate, the Chief gave Holmes a large number of cases, firm in the belief that only this would distract him in his grief.

It would not be long before Holmes would have an opportunity to salute Taft on his own behalf and that of the entire Court. In the fall 1929 term of the Court, Taft recognized that his health was failing, and the following February he resigned. In a letter dated February 10, and signed by all the justices, Holmes in what was for him a rare public display of his deepest emotion, offered this tribute.

> We call you Chief Justice still—for we can not give up the title by which we have known you all these later years and which you have made dear to us. We can not let you leave us without trying to tell you how dear you made it. You came to us from achievement in other fields and with the prestige of the illustrious place that you lately held and you showed us in new form your voluminous capacity for getting work done, your humor that smoothed the rough places, your golden heart that brought you love from every side and most of all from your brethren whose tasks you have made happy and light. We grieve at your illness, but your spirit has given life and impulse that will abide whether you are with us or away.[38]

Holmes had, indeed, captured in the frail envelope of language the essence of William Howard Taft as Chief Justice.

Justice Brandeis was a more formidable opponent of "massing" the Court. Whereas Holmes was neither liberal nor conservative—merely Holmesian and a coincidental Progressive, besides—Brandeis was one of the era's principal liberals. Through his profession as a lawyer and advocate before the High Court, he had dramatized the difference between judicial conservatism and political liberalism on numerous occasions. Brandeis was a Democrat as well. Taft and he had first clashed when, as legal counsel to Louis Glavis at the time of the Ballinger-Pinchot controversy, Brandeis made public the President's falsification of a date on a certain document that helped exonerate Ballinger. Taft's integrity had been more than slightly tarnished. When President Wilson nominated Brandeis to be an associate justice, Taft's reaction was extremely hostile. "It is one of the deepest wounds that I have suffered as an American and as a lover of the Constitution and a believer in progressive conservatism that such a man as Brandeis could be put on the court. . . . He is a muckraker, an emotionalist for his own purposes, a socialist . . . a man who has certain ideals . . . of great tenacity of purpose, and in my judgment of much power for evil."[39] This was a fearful condemnation. Furthermore, Taft lent his voice to the general clamor of opposition from "people of quality." Along with five other past presidents of the American Bar Association, he put his signature to a declaration that "Mr. Louis Brandeis is not a fit person to be a member of the Supreme Court of the United States."[40] Wilson's appointment, which Taft thought well calculated to win votes in the election year of 1916, was added reason to hate the President. In some part, Taft's animosity stemmed from his private hope, now doomed, that the Democratic chief executive would rise above party and name him to the Court as Taft had promoted White, a Democrat.

William Howard Taft was not inclined to carry a grudge forever—or, for that matter, for very long. He had forgiven Roosevelt, he was to succor Holmes, and his treatment of Brandeis was usually, if not always, in the same vein. Let Brandeis tell the story of their initial reconciliation as he conveyed it to his wife:

> Had an experience yesterday I did not expect to encounter in this life. As I was walking toward the Stoneleigh about 1 p.m. Taft and I met. There was a moment's hesitation and when he had almost passed, he stopped and said in a charming manner. 'Isn't this Justice Brandeis? I don't think we have ever met.' I answered, Yes, we met at Harvard after you returned from the Philippines.' He, at once, began to talk about my views on regularity of employment. After a moment I asked him to come in with me. He spent a half hour in 809, talking labor and War Labor Board experiences—was most confidential. I told him of the great service he had rendered the country by his action on the Labor Board and we parted with his saying in effect—he hoped we would meet often.[41]

Such an account perhaps says more about Taft than it does Brandeis. The date of the encounter was December 4, 1918; within three years the old adversaries would be colleagues on the bench.

A month after his appointment as chief justice, Brandeis wrote Taft a cordial note, congratulating him and stressing, among other things, the need to solve the problem of congestion in the district courts. In reply, Taft stated that he was looking forward "with pleasure to joint consideration and cooperation with you in this and all other matters of the Court."[42] The ice had been broken. In this exchange, and in their years together as justices, neither man proposed to forego scruple or surrender principle; but each was prepared to compromise on obiter dicta while holding securely to his own interpretation of the points of law. As Brandeis once told Felix Frankfurter: "I can't always dissent . . . sometimes . . . I acquiesce."[43] Taft had no difficulty appreciating Brandeis's virtues. He was a "very hard worker, who thinks much of the court and is anxious to have it consistent, and strong, and he pulls his weight in the boat." The Chief confided to his daughter: "I have come to like Brandeis very much indeed."[44]

After 1926, however, Taft's estimate of Brandeis altered drastically.

Reacting to the latter's dissent in an important case, he put Brandeis in that "class of people that have no loyalty to the Court and sacrifice almost everything to the gratification of their own publicity."[45] How to account for the Chief Justice's change of heart? As it was just that, a change of heart, his hostility sprung from the associate justice's accumulating dissenting opinions, particularly in those cases where he went against Taft's own preference in favor of private property. Apart from his altered attitude toward Brandeis (and Holmes), after 1926, Taft remained conservative in his outlook, determined to build a wall of protection against the enemies of private property who might come on the bench after he was gone.

Except for Holmes and Brandeis, the personnel of the Taft Court were conservative to the point of favoring reaction. One justice who might have tried Taft's patience by siding with the dissenters was John H. Clarke, resigned his seat in 1922 to work for the principles of the League of Nations. He was replaced by George Sutherland, a trustworthy Republican conservative and a justice the Chief came to lean on more and more. Only when Harlan Fiske Stone came to the Court and, soon thereafter, joined the Holmes-Brandeis connection was there much meaningful deviation from Taft's strategy to "mass" the Court. The others could almost always be relied on to constitute a conservative majority.

Friendship notwithstanding, no sooner had the fall 1921 term gotten underway than Taft and Holmes disagreed with one another. It might be a technical point of law, a provision of the Constitution when interpreted, or a fundamental of jurisprudence that brought them into opposition. No matter; the divergence was there, and cases argued and decided by the Court would make it evident. It may appear gratuitous to refer to examples of Chief Justice Taft's constitutional conservatism and Justice Holmes's liberalism as stated in their Court opinions of the 1920s. Nevertheless, it can prove useful within this context to cite such views so forthrightly expressed, because they appear to be definitive statements of their philosophies. And they are—but only to a point, as a case-by-case analysis is designed to point out.

For his part, Taft, in American Steel Foundries v. Tri-City Central Trades Council (1921), took the high ground in favor of property rights.[46] In retaliation for sharp cuts in wages, workers engaged in aggressive picketing on company property. Violence erupted, producing a knee-jerk reaction from Taft as he stiffened his sinews. He had long favored peaceful picketing as part of strike action, but in the real world of industrial disputes, distinctions between peaceful and violent picketing can be a matter of involvement and perspective. Taft, however, appeared to have a judicial rule of thumb: when in doubt, favor property rights. Incidentally, Holmes concurred with the Chief Justice in this case.

A similar sensitivity to property rights was registered the next year, in *United Mine Workers of America v. Coronado Coal Company* (1922), a case in which Taft reaffirmed the rule that unions might be actionable for damages arising from authorized union strike tactics.[47] Because many unions by that time had accumulated significant reserve funds, Taft's position was especially obnoxious to leaders of organized labor.

Holmes's liberal opinions in the *Gitlow* and *Olmstead* cases are well known. In the first, *Gitlow v. New York* (1925), the plaintiff had been found guilty under New York law of advocating criminal anarchy, and he appealed the state court decision to the Supreme Court of the United States.[48] The principal evidence submitted by the government was a document, "The Left Wing Manifesto," whose message was a call for class struggle, industrial strikes, revolt of the masses, and dictatorship of the proletariat. To a majority on the Court, this was no mere abstraction but a direct incitement to revolution. In dissent, Holmes allowed that "every idea is an incitement" but that from the facts of the case he was unable to discern any "clear and present danger." Once more he rejected the "bad tendency principle." Freedom of speech, to him, meant the freedom to utter the most detestable ideas, not simply those that were innocuous. When it came to freedom of speech, there were no absolutes beyond "the dominant force of the community."

Similarly, in *Schwimmer v. United States* (1928), Holmes took an anti-establishment stance.[49] Rosika Schwimmer had been denied citizenship because she had stated in her application that she could not in conscience take up arms in defense of the nation, as required by the Naturalization Act of 1906. The Court ruled that it was a fundamental duty of a citizen to defend the country if so called upon. Holmes's dissent was strongly personalized. He defended Schwimmer as a woman of superior intelligence, a desirable citizen. As for bearing arms, she was a woman, past fifty years of age; thus the requirement was academic, a non-issue. Only at the close of his dissent did Holmes introduce the argument that "the principle of free thought . . . freedom for the thought that we hate" is germane. The justice told one admirer of his ruling that "it was moral sympathy, not legal judgment that led to praise of him."[50] In fact, Holmes had made the moral judgment, the law was clear. In the privacy of his correspondence, his intimation that Schwimmer's flamboyant declaration of atheism made the Court's decision against her easier to pronounce also serves as a clue to his own attitude of support.

Truax v. Corrigan (1921) was Taft's first major opinion, but it also constitutes his first sharp difference in judgment with the views of Holmes.[51] The case grew out of a labor dispute between the owners of "The English Kitchen" restaurant, in Bisbee, Arizona, and some of its employees. A picket line was established surrounding the place of business which turned out to be a staunch campaign by the workers to discourage customers from entering the restaurant. The owners contended that, as a consequence, daily receipts dropped from an average of $150 a day to $75. "Great and irreparable injury" resulted. Ordinarily, an injunction would have been sought to restrain or prohibit the picketing; but the state legislature had enacted a law greatly restricting the state courts from proceeding in this fashion except in an emergency. No emergency could be said to exist. The legal issue as the case came before the Supreme Court centered on whether the state law violated the due process clause of the Fourteenth Amendment. Was the law not a denial of the protection afforded property from interference by the state? Speaking for the Court in what was to be a five-to-four decision, Taft ruled in favor of the right of the property owners to be protected against application of the Arizona statute. Taft's opinion contains three key passages. Taken together, they leave no doubt of the Chief Justice's commitment to protection of property, given the circumstances in this case. Taft stated plainly that "a law which operates to make lawful such a wrong as is described in plaintiff's complaint deprives the owner of the business and the premises of his property . . . can not be held valid under the Fourteenth Amendment." Granting the proposition that property rights are not absolute, Taft insisted that "the legislative power of a State can only be exerted in subordination to the fundamental principles of right and justice which the guaranty of the due process clause of the Fourteenth Amendment is intended to preserve, and that a purely arbitrary or capricious exercise of that power whereby a wrongful and highly injurious invasion of property rights, as here, is practically sanctioned and the owner stripped of all real remedy, is wholly at variance with those principles." He went on to argue: "To give operation to a statute whereby serious losses inflicted by such unlawful means are in effect remedies, is, we think, to disregard fundamental rights of liberty and property and to deprive the person suffering the loss of due process." It is easy enough to summarize by saying that Taft's major premise— property rights—is the bedrock of our civilization and therefore of the law, and such was the heart of the matter. At this stage in Justice Holmes's evolution as a civil libertarian, it is less readily predictable how he would view the majority's appeal to the due process clause. (One can think ahead to *United Zinc Company* v. *Britt,* decided the next year.) In any event, Holmes disagreed with the majority in what was a concise yet pithy answer to Taft's lengthy arguments. In particular, he objected to "calling a business 'property' [making] it seem like land" and leading up to the conclusion that that "statute cannot substantially cut down the advantages of ownership existing before the statute was passed." But it is Holmes's jurisprudential retort that carries the greater force. "There is nothing that I more deprecate than the use of the Fourteenth Amendment beyond the absolute compulsion of its words to prevent the making of social experiments that an important part of the community desires, in the insulated chambers afforded by the several States, even though the experiments may seem futile or even noxious to me and to those whose judgment I most respect." And, finally, Holmes went on to remark that he agreed "with the more elaborate exposition of my brothers, Pitney and Brandeis, and in their conclusion." It would appear that Taft and Holmes may have been setting out on a collision course that could play havoc with the work (and, quite possibly, the reputation) of the Court in public life.

The impasse threatened by the outcome of *Truax* v. *Corrigan* did not materialize, at least not immediately and while the Court concerned itself with issues of trade and commerce. When it came to interpreting the commerce clause, three cases in particular demonstrated concurrence rather than dispute: *Stafford* v. *Wallace* (1922), *City of Chicago Board of Trade* v. *Olsen* (1923), and *Bailey* v. *Drexel Furniture Company* (1922).[52] The *Stafford* case grew out of a law passed by Congress in 1921, the Packers and Stockyards Act. To prevent meatpackers from manipulating the prices of cattle to their advantage, Congress saw fit to regulate their business, and, because their monopoly was aided by control of the stockyards, the latter facilities were brought under the law. Writing the majority opinion, Taft noted how "thousands of livestock arrived daily by carloads and train lots and must be promptly sold and disposed of, moved out to give place to the constantly flowing traffic." These animals came from all points on the compass, from nearby states and those far away. To put it plainly, they were moving in interstate commerce. Because the packing business controlled a vital part of the nation's food supply, Taft maintained that it was clothed with a public interest so that the law treated the various stockyards and packing houses as "great national public utilities." Both *Munn* v. *Illinois* (1877) and *Swift and Company* v. *United States* (1904) were cited with Taft concluding that the latter case created "a fixed rule of the Court in the construction and application of the commerce clause." By use of such arguments as "commerce among the states is not a technical legal conception but a practical one, drawn from the course of business," the Chief Justice, given the facts as presented, had few if any qualms about the exercise of federal legislative authority. His opinion might well be thought of as a "progressive" ruling, the Swift case coming very early in that reform movement. Justice Holmes was in agreement. As has already been remarked, Holmes complimented the Chief for his masterful language as he defined the span of control the commerce clause gave Congress.

Broadly conceived, *Chicago Board of Trade* v. *Olsen* was an affirmation of the ruling in the Stafford case, with Taft again writing the opinion. Quoting extensively from arguments he had advanced earlier, he revealed an expert's understanding of the flow of business at the "greatest grain market in the world." Congress had acted wisely by forbidding trading in grain futures except when supervised by the secretary of agriculture. The regulation was based on the assumption that the public interest would be threatened otherwise. Nor was Taft unaware of the temptations to manipulate grain futures, which could produce a ripple effect across state lines. As he pointed out, "a futures market lends itself to manipulation much more readily than a cash market." The 1921 act in question did nothing more than make explicit the prohibitions of the Sherman Anti-trust Act. Holmes being the "coincidental" Progressive he was, had no trouble agreeing with Taft's line of reasoning.

What is surprising is Holmes's position in *Bailey* v. *Drexel Furniture Company*. The Child Labor Tax Law passed in 1919 was the second congressional attempt to restrain the practice of employing children under the age of fourteen when engaged in the manufacture of products traded in interstate commerce. The ten percent tax on yearly net profits was designed to discourage this social abuse. Despite his position in the above cases, Taft drew a line on extending the scope of Congressional taxing power to permit this kind of social engineering. Such laws might be constitutional, he thought, if enacted at the state level; but they could not be part of the laws of the United States. To do so would invade the reserved powers of the states as provided by the Tenth Amendment. The tax was seen not as a levy on a commodity moving in interstate trade but merely on the circumstances under which the product was manufactured.

Understandably, Taft fell back on the ruling in *Hammer* v. *Dagenhart*. "The analogy of the Dagenhart Case is clear," he said. Nor did he find germane the arguments in *McGray* v. *United States* (1904). In contrast, the position enunciated by John Marshall in *McCulloch* v. *Maryland* was quoted to good effect: "Should Congress adopt measures which are prohibited by the Constitution . . . it would become the painful duty of this tribunal . . . to say that such an act was not the law of the land." Only Justice Clarke dissented, Holmes giving consent by his silence. Yet Holmes's attitude is not altogether surprising. His judgment in *Hammer* v. *Dagenhart* was hardly vigorous. Holmes's famous "if" usage—"if we were to introduce our own moral conceptions where in my opinion they do not belong"—found him on the horns of a legal/moral dilemma. He did not really believe that morality should play a part in adjudication. True, he *did* vote to uphold the Keating-Owen Child Labor Act in what was hardly a ringing endorsement of the will of Congress. Had Holmes rethought the matter? None of his major biographers addresses this possibility. It has been suggested that he simply went along with Brandeis, that they "sometimes suppressed their dissents for tactical reasons." Brandeis's motivation aside, Holmes the Outspoken rarely thought in tactical terms. Perhaps he had come round more fully to the position that morality had no place in the processes of the law. Yet this is difficult to accept when the issues before the 1920s Court concerned civil liberties. Does it not convey a moral feeling about the law to write, as he did in *Olmstead* v. *United States* that it is "a less evil that some criminals should escape than the government should play an ignoble part?"[53] The resort to the word *evil* resonates morality. Yet, while concurring in the Bailey case, he declined the opportunity to speak out in support of a law aimed at achieving a noble purpose.

Adkins v. *Children's Hospital* (1922) occupies an important place in the annals of the 1920s Court if for no other reason than dissents by Taft and Holmes upholding the minimum wage law for the District of Columbia.[54] What was there in the facts of the case or the wording of the law that caused them to see almost eye to eye? Or was there a larger, more remote consideration adding to our understanding that would seem to be required in light of the positions taken in Bailey? After all, setting minimum wages for women was akin to protecting no less vulnerable children from exploitation. Once social considerations are introduced in the judgment it is, oddly enough, easier to appreciate Taft's about-face than the position of Holmes. Both dissents could and did cite precedents, *Muller* v. *Oregon* and *Bunting* v. *Oregon* thereby giving them constitutional respectability. In economic matters Taft and Holmes had revealed varying degrees of commitment to sociological jurisprudence—admittedly, Holmes more so than Taft. Beyond these aspects of judgment stand the differing personalities of the two justices. Taft was more likely to be moved by the plight of women involved in hospital work than would Holmes. Taft had fathered children and had come to know grandchildren. Holmes eschewed parenthood. Taft was warmhearted, Holmes was not. Taft had seen more of life as it is lived. After his terrible experiences during the Civil War, Holmes became detached.

In the Adkins case, the majority of the Court concluded that liberty of contract had been unconstitutionally invaded by the minimum wage law. As much as Taft favored property rights, exceptions could be made, and such an exception was called for here. This interpretation of Taft's judgment may seem shadowy, but it must be remembered that there are occasions when the humanity of a judge overpowers a judicial philosophy. In assessing Holmes's position it is useful to quote him on two counts. He wrote that the power of Congress in passing the legislation "seems absolutely free of doubt." Then he added: "the end, to remove conditions leading to ill health, immorality, and the destruction of the race, no one would deny to be within the scope of constitutional legislation." Reference to "ill health" and the "destruction of the race" are strongly sociological arguments, but sandwiched between them is "immorality," a reminder of Holmes's inability to separate himself completely from his Puritan past.

Both Bailey and Adkins carried a certain amount of moral baggage, whereas most cases coming before the Court in the first half of the 1920s emanated from the world of business. However, three additional cases invite examination for what they tell of the Taft-Holmes differences over the meaning of the law. Pennsylvania Coal Company v. Mahon (1922), United Zinc Company v. Britt (1922), and Bartels v. Iowa (1923) are studies in contrast and comparison.[55]

Holmes's conservative instincts were in full evidence in his majority opinion in Pennsylvania Coal Company v. Mahon. In it, he sided with a number of "known" conservatives, including the Chief Justice; more significantly, he broke ranks with Brandeis. The issue in the case dealing with a state law was fairly clear-cut: May property rights be restricted in the public interest, that is, may the right of a company to mine coal be maintained even though the mining operation caused cave-ins to private dwellings located above the coal fields? Holmes moved to strike down the law, insisting on the rights of the corporation. His argument is fairly hard-nosed. "In ordinary private affairs the public interest does not warrant much of this kind of state interference. A source of damage to such a house is not a public nuisance even if similar damage is inflicted on others in different places. The damage is not common or public. . . . Furthermore the statute is not justified as a protection of personal safety." Later in his opinion, Holmes retreated to one of his favorite whipping boys—generalities. "The general rule at least is, that while property may be regulated to a certain extent, if regulation goes too far it will be recognized as taking." Writing to Pollock, Holmes insisted that he was not speaking in generalities, but only with respect to this particular case. He also told his English friend that everybody seemed to have misgivings about the police power involved; but he believed he had delivered "a compact statement of the real facts of the law and as such sure to arouse opposition for want of the customary soft phrase."[56] And, to Laski he said: "I confess to feeling as much confidence as I often do."[57]

Adding to the impression that Holmes was a closet conservative is his position in *United Zinc Company* v. *Britt*. Another way to look at the Britt decision is that it badly tarnished Holmes's liberal reputation. It should also be noted that, in this case, the Supreme Court reversed a decision of a circuit court of appeals. Two children, aged eight and eleven, died as a result of swimming in a pool of water that had been poisoned by sulfuric acid. The company knew of the hazardous condition and had made no effort to fence it off. Speaking for the Court, and no less for himself, Holmes reasoned as follows:

> If the children had been adults they would have had no case. They would have been trespassers and the owner of the land would have owed no duty to remove even hidden dangers; it would have been entitled to assume that they would have obeyed the law and not trespass. . . . Infants have no greater right to go upon other people's land than adults and the mere fact that they are infants imposes no duty upon the landowners to expect them and to prepare for their safety.

The life of the law in this case seems to be logic after all. Something of that sort may have been on his mind when Holmes confided to Pollock regarding the Britt case: "my brother Clarke uttered a larmoyant dissent that seemed to me more sentiment and rhetoric than reason." And, he added, "the C J and Day agreed with him but I suspect on reasoning of their own."[58]

What, then, were the elements of Justice Clarke's dissent with which Taft, lacking evidence to the contrary, was likely to have agreed? Clarke began by noting that courts have sharply divided as to the principles of law applied to "attractive nuisances." He was quick to point out, however, that the unanimous decision of the Supreme Court in *Railroad Company v. Stout* (1873) found for culpable negligence in a similar case where children were involved. Furthermore, in *Union Pacific Ry. Co. v. McDonald* (1893), the principle invoked in the Stout case was reaffirmed. Clarke, and presumably Taft, felt he was on firm constitutional ground. He proceeded to describe in great detail in appearance and layout of the pool of water and its surroundings. Located close to a town of some 10,000 inhabitants, the pool was in a field that had criss-crossing paths. Yet there was no fence or warning sign to take the children's attention. Clarke admitted that if the boys had merely drowned, there could be no recovery. Testimony indicated that the pool seemed to be filled with clear water, and its poisonous character could not have been known to the youngsters. It was, in short, an attractive nuisance. To add strength to his constitutional argument, Clarke called attention to *City of Pekin v. McMahon*, an Illinois Supreme Court case which held the city liable for the death of a child under similar circumstances. The Illinois court had acted on the strength of the Stout decision. Contending that allowances should be made for the instincts and conduct of children "of tender years," Clarke concluded his opinion by writing that it was a "harsh rule which makes trespassers of little children." Holmes was correct in describing the prose of the dissent as sentimental. In this instance, however, it is more likely that Taft was moved to agree with Clarke, based on clear-cut Court precedent. The difference between Taft and Holmes stands out, nonetheless.[59]

One of the home-front reactions to U.S. involvement in World War I can be identified in laws prohibiting the teaching of foreign languages in American elementary schools before a student had passed through the eighth grade. Three Midwestern states—Nebraska, Iowa, and Ohio—put such statutes in effect. Was the motivation anti-German, since Germany was the enemy and German was one of the proscribed languages? Or was it a manifestation of xenophobia, a reaction against immigrants and their ways rendered most dramatic by their non-English speech? On the other hand, the motivation of the states may have been more positive, insisting on English at an early school age to produce a desired assimilation of such people into American ways; certainly using English every day would facilitate attaining that laudable objective. Whatever the reasons behind such a law, suits were brought in all three states, challenging their constitutionality on the grounds that a violation of the due process clause of the Fourteenth Amendment had occurred. Justice McReynolds, speaking for the majority in *Meyers v. Nebraska* (1923), began his opinion by quoting from the North West Ordinance, that "the means of education shall forever be encouraged" and that the mere knowledge of the German language can not reasonably be regarded as harmful.[60] Heretofore, it had been commonly looked upon as helpful and desirable." (Incidentally, German was the only language specified in the case as being prohibited.) McReynolds observed that, by learning English, foreigners could more readily aspire to American ideas which was an important public objective." In consequence, the "State may do much, go very far, in order to improve the quality of its citizens . . . but they can not be coerced by methods which conflict with the Constitution—a desirable end can not be promoted by a prohibited means." Furthermore, freedom to teach as well as freedom to learn was central to the issue as it was raised.

Taft concurred in this ruling; but, in a companion case, *Bartels v. Iowa*, handed down at the same time, Holmes chose to uphold the state statute, at least in Iowa.[61] Without denying the desirability of citizens of the United States speaking a common tongue, Holmes feared that the means provided did not deny to teachers or students their liberty under the due process clause. He phrased his objection this way: "I am not prepared to say that it is unreasonable to provide that in his early years he [the student] should not hear and speak only English at school. But if it is reasonable it is not an undue restriction of either teacher or student." In conclusion, he added: "I am unable to say that the Constitution of the United States prevents this experience from being tried." Referencing the issue to Holmes's judicial philosophy, liberty was pitted against the right of the state to police its education system, with the latter principle the prevailing one.

Looking back over the rulings in these three cases, we see that Holmes had argued against the property rights of the individual as protected by a state law and was supported by the Chief Justice. He had invoked the law of trespass over the rights of children to be warned about the dangers implicit in an "attractive nuisance," a finding Taft rejected. Finally, Holmes insisted on a state legislature's right to control its system of education at the cost of denying application of the due process clause of the Fourteenth Amendment, a case which found Taft in disagreement. If one is keeping score at this point, Holmes's liberalism is hardly distinguishable from Taft's conservatism, startling as that may sound.

An issue distinct from disagreements over the application of the com-

merce clause or the protection of civil liberties surfaced in 1923, in
Myers v. *United States*, reargued in 1925 and decided in 1926, and *Ex
parte Grossman* argued in 1924 and decided the next year.[62] The dates
cited are important to bear in mind because the points at law in question—namely, the extent of presidential pardoning power and that of
removing subordinates from office are closely intertwined. Majority decisions in the cases were delivered by the Chief Justice, and it becomes
clear from the positions he took that his experience as President influenced his judgment.

First *Ex parte Grossman*. Philip Grossman had been accused in U.S.
district court of violating the National Prohibition Act. A restraining
order had been placed on his business activity, distribution of alcoholic
beverages, which he ignored. He was arrested, found guilty of contempt
of court, and sentenced to pay of fine of $1,000 and to be jailed for a
period of one year. The President of the United States issued a pardon
and commuted the prison sentence, provided the fine was paid. Grossman accepted the pardon and paid the fine. The pardon notwithstanding, the district court committed Grossman to jail to serve out the year's
sentence. An appeal was made to the Supreme Court. Taft wrote an
erudite opinion in which he defended the pardoning power of the president. He cited Article II, Section 2 of the Constitution as the basis of
his decision, to wit: the President "shall have the power to grant Re-
prieves and Pardons for Offenses against the United States, except in
cases of Impeachment." Taft took the opportunity to show that the
executive authority involved was not only a part of the U.S. Constitution, but that it was embedded in English common law. The sticking
point in the case was whether contempt of court was a crime or an
offense against the United States. Taft was to contend, "That which
offends the dignity and authority of the federal courts such as an intentional effort to defeat their decrees justifying punishment violates a law
of the United States." It was as simple as that to the Chief Justice who,
not long before, had been the Chief Executive. As he bent to his task,
the former President seemed to relish the opportunity to display his
understanding of the issue raised, considered in the light of history,
while at the same time defending presidential prerogative for its own
sake. In closing, Taft insisted that the pardoning power was not a matter
of undermining the authority of the courts; such a purpose could not be
further from his mind. Whereupon he made a remarkable concession to
human frailty when it came to enforcing the law:

Is it unreasonable to provide for the possibility that the personal element may sometimes enter into a summary judgment pronounced by a judge who thinks his authority is flouted or denied? May it not be fairly said that in order to avoid possible mistakes, undue prejudice or endless severity, the chance of pardon should exist at least as much in favor of a person convicted by a judge without a jury as in favor of one convicted in a jury trial?

One almost has to remind oneself that this is Judge William Howard Taft who uttered these words.

If hard cases make bad law, as Holmes was known to contend, do cases of no great consequence to the individuals involved or to the nation make good law? *Myers* v. *United States* raises this question. Myers was removed from his first-class postmaster's position three months before the expiration of his four-year appointment. He sued in the Court of Claims for the salary he thought due him subsequent to his dismissal. That Court agreed that Myers was not guilty of laches but rejected his claim for salary compensation. Before examining Taft's opinion in support of the Claims Court's judgment, it is important to point out that his administrative style when President is best described as strict chain of command. He believed in straight-line, unencumbered authority.

The best example of this is to be found in his handling of the Ballinger-Pinchot controversy in 1910. Pinchot had stepped out of line by going over the head of his superior. This was behavior unacceptable to the President, and Pinchot was dismissed from office. Taft was to pay dearly for this, but he could not be persuaded to do otherwise. Accountability from top to bottom was basic to effective administration. In the case of Myers, he had been removed from his postmastership by the postmaster general, an action taken at the direction of the President. Myers had refused a demand for his resignation and was thus dismissed. Taft began his opinion by focusing on that part of the Constitution which states that Presidents have the power to remove officers in the executive departments of the United States who had received their appointment with the advice and consent of the Senate. As it happened, Myers had made no appeal to the Senate which, under a Congressional act of 1876, he was free to do. Taft made a painstaking review of the relevant portions of Articles II and III of the Constitution. Then he referred to the history of the debates in the Constitutional Convention, which he said showed that it was the intention of the Convention to give to the executive uninhibited powers of removal. Taft, in fact, gave a long, in-depth history lesson as he commented on Farrand's *Records* of the Convention. How could the President be held accountable that the laws be faithfully executed if his hands were to be tied by asking for senatorial approval to remove, which might or might not be forthcoming? *Parsons v. United States* was cited to support the removal power, as well as the Judiciary Act of 1789. He also called attention to a wartime act of 1862, regarding the power of the President to remove military officers whose work was deemed unsuitable. In his development of this full-scale defense of the presidential removal power, Taft wrote seventy pages of history, precedent, tradition, and common sense exhibiting throughout a mastery of fact which, when combined with a confidence born of experience as civil governor in the Philippines, Secretary of War, and President of the United States, made this opinion his greatest state paper. Both Brandeis and McReynolds entered lengthy dissents, to which Holmes gave his agreement, praising their exhaustive research; but he added his own words. Rarely did theory on Holmes's part so muddy the water. He wrote:

> We have to deal with an office that owes its existence to Congress and that Congress may abolish tomorrow. . . . Congress alone confers on the President the power to appoint to it and at any time may transfer that power to other hands. With such power over its own creation I have no more trouble in believing that Congress has power to prescribe a term of life for it free from any interference than I have in accepting the undoubted power of Congress to decree its end.

Such resort to theory which conjures up the unimaginable—that is, that Congress would decree the end of the Post Office Department—is logical, but in the real world of the 1920s, it was hardly a tenable one.

Civil liberties cases were among the highlights of the work of the 1920s court. They became magnified by reason of the belief that the justices were deeply divided by the issues brought before them. It is not always clear how defining these differences of legal opinion actually were; but a sampling of them may convey a sense of the divisions that afflicted the Court from the very beginning. No sooner had Taft taken the helm than *Leach v. Carlile Postmaster* (1921) came up for judgment.[63] The U.S. Post Office had refused to transmit literature for "Organo Tablets" on the grounds that to do so constituted fraudulent representation of the medicine. In essence, it was a matter of free speech versus prior censorship. Justice Clarke, speaking for the Court majority that included the chief justice, affirmed the decision of the lower court to exclude such literature from the mails. Clarke's reasoning was cautious but conclusive. "The question decided by the lower courts was not that the substance the appellant was selling was entirely worthless as a medicine, as to which there was some conflict in the evidence, but that it was so far from being a panacea which he was advertising . . . that by so advertising it he was perpetuating a fraud upon the public." Holmes issued a dissent with which Brandeis concurred. In part, it read: "I do not suppose that any one would say that freedom of written speech is less protected by the First Amendment than the freedom of the spoken word. Therefore I can not understand by what authority Congress undertakes to authorize anyone to determine in advance, on the grounds before us, that certain words shall not be uttered. Even those who interpret the Amendment most strictly agree that it was intended to prevent previous restraint." *Leach* v. *Carlile Postmaster* was not a case of great pith or moment; yet it demonstrated potential divisions among the brethren when civil liberties were involved.

Justice Holmes spoke for a unanimous court in *United States* v. *Sullivan* (1927), in which the protections offered by the Fifth Amendment came under scrutiny.[64] Sullivan was engaged in the illicit liquor trade from which he enjoyed a profitable income. He was sentenced in federal district court for wilfully refusing to file a return of net income as required by the Revenue Act of 1921. Counsel for the defendant urged that "the obvious intent of the Fifth Amendment is that no one shall be compelled to be the means of exposing his own criminality. This privilege is for the protection of the innocent as well as the guilty." In one way, Holmes made short work of this construction of the Fifth Amendment: "We are of the opinion that the protection of the Fifth Amendment was pressed too far." That terse statement would have been sufficient to dispose of Sullivan's defense; but Holmes proceeded to isolate and discuss a legal technicality. In effect, he said that the defendant should have invoked the Fifth Amendment on his income tax return, but this could not be ruled on because he had refused to file any tax return at all. Such a move would have been an "extreme if not extravagant" use of the Fifth Amendment, but he thought that it would have made an interesting test case. That the Chief Justice appreciated this latter possibility is unlikely.

Nixon v. *Herndon* (1927) brought two postulates into possible conflict, more troublesome for Holmes than for Taft.[65] Judicial restraint had been one of Holmes's guidelines so that only in extreme circumstances should the Court interfere with the will of the state lawmakers. As Holmes stated in this opinion: "States may do a good deal of classifying that it is difficult to believe rational, but there are limits." In *Nixon* v. *Herndon*, the limits had been significantly exceeded—namely, a denial by the State of Texas to the plaintiff of the right to vote in a Democratic primary election. In the 1920s the primary election there was the determining election because of the iron grip Democrats had on the electoral process. The 1923 Texas law was unequivocal: "In no event shall a negro be eligible to participate in a Democratic party primary election held in the state of Texas." Having been denied that right, Nixon sued. Holmes was direct and unambiguous in addressing the situation. "The question at law is whether the statute can be sustained . . . the answer does not seem to be open to doubt." Holmes went on to state that it was "hard to imagine a more direct and obvious infringement of the Fourteenth [Amendment]. That Amendment while it applies to all, was passed as we know to protect blacks from discrimination against them." Quoting generously from *Buchanan* v. *Warley* (1909), the Texas law was a clear-cut denial of the equal protection of the law. "What this is but declaring that the law in the State shall be the same for black and for white, that all persons, whether colored or white, shall stand equal before the laws of the State." Taft, to be sure, agreed with Holmes as did all the Court. But it causes one to wonder why the Chief Justice did not himself write the opinion as the outcome of the case was assured by the arrogance of the state law, quite apart from its unconstitutionality. Had he wanted to showcase his intolerance for this kind of state action, a Taft majority opinion would have reflected well on him. Or had he conceded civil liberties cases to Holmes and/or Brandeis to promote good feelings in a court seemingly more rent by internal divisions than in years before?

Two historic cases, *Buck* v. *Bell* (1926) and *Olmstead* v. *United States* (1927), work to sharpen the images of Taft and Holmes as upholders of the law.[66] Appropriately, the dichotomy lies across a conservative-liberal axis, although differing versions of judicial restraint also figure in the rulings. Holmes wrote the *Buck* v. *Bell* opinion, with only Justice Butler dissenting. Taft spoke for the majority in Olmstead, with Holmes doing a brief but pointed dissent. Brandeis weighed in with a lengthy, reasoned opinion, with Butler and Stone supplying further opposition to the majority opinion. The Chief Justice had failed—miserably, it might be said—in his efforts to mass the Court; but by 1927 this was an established trend. In each of the cases, Holmes would utter some of his most quoted Court language, which caused controversy at the time and in the critical literature of later years. Taft, in turn, was his typical self:

offering no separate opinion when he concurred, but going all out when he was determined that law and order must be guarded vigilantly.

Buck v. *Bell* grew out of a Virginia state law that provided sexual sterilization of inmates of institutions supported by the state who were affected with a hereditary form of insanity or imbecility. Carrie Buck was the daughter of a feebleminded mother and the mother of a feeble-minded child. She was housed in the State Colony of Epileptics and Feebleminded. The state proposed to subject her to a salpingectomy, as called for in the statute. The attorney for Buck argued that such an operation was illegal because it violated "her constitutional right to bodily integrity" and was "therefore repugnant to the due process clause of the Fourteenth Amendment," as well as the equal protection of the law. No standard had been set, according to Buck's attorney. Where, he asked, would the sterilization of the unfit stop? "In the name of science new classes will be added, even races may be brought within the scope of the law and the worst form of tyranny practiced." These were emotionally charged words, with profound ethical implications. Holmes's position, as has sometimes been overlooked, was concise and carefully stated. He explained the various safeguards the Virginia law included to avoid hasty and thoughtless action. With some display of emotion, and no doubt with an unspoken reference to the Civil War dead, he wrote: "We have seen more than once that the public welfare may call upon the best citizens for their lives. It would be strange if it could not call upon those who already sap the strength of the state for lesser sacrifices . . . in order to prevent our being swamped with incompetence." This was a measured line of reasoning. His final, summing up statement—"Three generations of imbeciles are enough"— came across as pontification. The practice of judicial restraint, allowing the state law to stand, combined with contemporary eugenics with the ghosts of the Civil War dead embedded in his subconscious, was to wring from Holmes this savage aphorism. Even friendly biography has called his position in *Buck* v. *Bell* troubling.[67] It is also troubling to think that Taft did not choose to write a concurring opinion, based on the law alone and free of personal animus.

By common, if not universal, consent the Eighteenth Amendment and its enabling legislation was one of the great misadventures in American law. Enacted according to all the constitutional prescriptions, the law was difficult and probably impossible to enforce. Whether it accurately reflected the will of the people may be a matter of dispute, but there is no doubt that Prohibition nurtured organized crime, adding a new and baleful feature to American society. At about the same time, the use of the telephone for business and government purposes was growing quickly, as well as for the more affluent residents of towns and cities. Thus, if organized crime could flourish because of the unenforcability of Prohibition, developing technology gave to law officers a new means of detecting crime and prosecuting criminals who increasingly used the telephone system to engage in illegal businesses. Such large considerations provide the context for *Olmstead v. United States* (1928).

Chief Justice Taft, writing for the majority in what was a five-to-four decision, contended that the tapping of telephone lines of those suspected of violating the National Prohibition Law in order to get proof of such criminal actions did not violate the Fourth Amendment's protection against unwarranted searches and seizures, nor the Fifth Amendment's protection against self-incrimination. In assaying Taft's opinion it is important to guard against latter-day mob activity and confine our consideration to the mores of the 1920s. Taft underscored the magnitude of the conspiracy at the center of which was Olmstead, along with other "investors" in the "business." He also described the gathering of evidence which had gone on for several months and reviewed the particulars of the two amendments in question. Numerous court rulings were but the determining rule Taft identified as the common law dictum, namely, that the admissibility of evidence was not affected by the methods whereby it was obtained. Holmes's counterstatement is well known and virtually enshrined: "We have to choose and for my part I think it less an evil that some criminals should escape than that the Government should commit an ignoble act." In so saying, it appeared that Holmes was the one stuck in the nineteenth century, an era devoid both of organized crime and wide usage of an instrument like the telephone. Was he expressing the same mentality, derived from a more genteel time, when it was bad form for a gentleman to read another's mail? Which is not to say that Taft had a superior grasp of what the future held as he fell back on one of the hoary precepts of the common law. But what Taft did recognize was, the common law rule could be rendered inapplicable were Congress to enact legislation updating it to meet the realities of communication in the twentieth century. In other words, the Chief Justice was exercising his own version of judicial restraint not in the presence of a law passed by Congress but in the absence of such an enactment. It was not the business of the court to substitute its will for that of the national legislature.

The visions Taft and Holmes entertained of the law were often strikingly different, yet similar enough, if not identical, to undermine the stereotypes whereby each has been praised or denounced. Their years together on the 1920s Court were witness to an occasional role reversal rendering a strict line of demarcation between conservative-liberal, activist-restrainist, or both, elusive and perhaps not especially helpful. Taft's Court record has prompted a characterization of him as "chameleon-like," alternating shades of judicial coloring.[68] Whether such an estimate is simply an effort to describe the variety of the chief justice's opinions or to impute to him a inconsistency of judging, it may be compared to the verdict that "Holmesian" best attests to the singularity of Holmes's opinions over the full course of his Court tenure. Holmes was known to change his stripes, depending on the specifics of the case being considered at any given time. Yet somehow, "Taftian" or "Taft-like" cannot claim to convey a clear image of the chief justice. No doubt, the difference, in effect, lies in the men themselves. Intellectually, morally, jurisprudentially, Taft is a much less complex person than Holmes—intellectual adventurer, moral pilgrim and judicial skeptic.

Born only fifteen years apart and offspring of the scientific revolution, they possessed values and a way of thinking that could be sharply opposed. But not always so. And why is that? To begin with, their philosophies of life were materialist. Theirs was a materialist world, subject to the forces of change and adaptation and capable of producing a high civilization made so by reason of security of life and property. Whether Taft is best categorized as a Reform Darwinist or Holmes as a practicing pragmatist makes little difference when it comes to the control man could exercise over environment to attain not the heavenly city of the eighteenth-century philosophers but the brave new world of science regnant. Much is made of Taft's seemingly one-dimensional attitude toward the sanctity of private property. To him, civilization was the equivalent of a capitalist society. But how much did this diverge from Holmes's view of his world? Writing to Canon Sheehan in 1912, he told his friend about the address he had recently delivered at Williams College. In his account he comes across as a no-nonsense capitalist, as the following observations bear out. "Most people think dramatically not quantitatively . . . 85 percent of the total product here and in England was consumed by the people with not more than $1,000 (£200) a year—the whole expense of government and the modest luxuries of the many accounting for the remaining 15 per cent." "It is not popular to tell the crowd that they now have substantially all there is, and that the war on capitalism is the fight of the striking group against all the other producers." "As long as people stop with questions of ownership and money . . . they are sure to think fallacies."[69] It was almost as though capitalism were natural to the socioeconomy and socialism a futile gesture. Sumner's dictum about the absurd effort to make the world over resonated in Holmes's outlook.

In the history of the nation, capitalism and the Constitution were closely linked. Holmes was more reserved in his admiration for Chief Justice Marshall than was Taft, but he recognized the obvious, that Marshall, through his dominance of the Court for some thirty years, cemented capitalism and the Constitution in an unbreakable, mutually supporting bond. Responding to the times and its varied and conflicting intellectual currents, Taft approached the Constitution in the spirit of Reform Darwinism. Like Sumner, he accepted the broad outline or scheme of things as settled and beyond dispute. What Nature was to Sumner, capitalism/constitutional was to Taft; within that system the struggle for change was to take place. Such changes that were necessary or even inevitable could be dealt with under, and within, the parameters laid down by the great law. The dynamics of man in society, dynamics Taft accepted as natural to the human condition, must remain within its purview. It is incorrect to say that Taft deplored change. In his political years he had a respectable record as a Progressive, a movement that looked to managed change, and thus improvement. His time as chief justice would do the same.

To understand Holmes in relation to Taft, it is important to appreciate both the pragmatist and the ethical relativist in his dealing with the law, both constitutional and statute. It must be added that Holmes was at least one part Social Darwinism and one part Malthusian. "I believe that Malthus was right in his fundamental notion. . . . Every society is founded on the death of men. . . . I shall think that socialism begins to be entitled to serious treatment when and not before it takes life in hand and prevents the continuance of the unfit."[70] Holmes had strong opinions and expressed them trenchantly; as such, they are immensely quotable. Many times, they could be highly personal, not necessarily shared by all who heard them. Taft too could be outspoken, based on his feelings. His ad hominem attack on Brandeis in 1916 is a chilling example. Their values—those of Taft and Holmes, even when it came to judging—carried a personal inflection. Taft recognized this in an oblique way in Ex parte Grossman when he conceded "the possibility that a personal element may sometimes enter into a summary judgment pronounced by a judge." It seems certain he would not have excluded himself from such a possibility.

Holmes allowed even more of the personal element in the opening passages of *The Common Law*, wherein "even the prejudices which judges share with their fellow men," may influence the character of the law.[71] What is the reverse of prejudices? The answer is "preferences," which may have an equally powerful pull on the mind or heart. Realistically, people, including judges and including Taft and Holmes, are well supplied with both. Holmes went so far as to claim among the sources of the law were "intuitions of public policy, avowed or unconscious."[72] "Intuition" is hardly scientific and cannot pretend to be. Prejudices, preferences, intuitions come both from a reading of history and philosophy and a response to the contemporary climate of opinion: intellectual, moral, economic, political or popular. In consequence, for Taft, the law was an instrument to control the extent and pace of what he recognized as a changing society. Holmes inclined to treat law as an instrument to permit such changes as society expressly preferred. Each man was an instrumentalist according to his own lights. They could, and did, agree and disagree on how the law was used.

To offer this reflection is not to prescind from the differing interpretations of the law separating the chief justice from "the venerable justice." It is, instead, to rise above their opposing positions and thereby identify in them and their work variants of post-formalism in the American legal tradition. In the process of growth, Holmes was more advanced in his thinking than Taft. But, just as Holmes's rulings in matters of civil liberties gained ground in the decades that followed, so Taft's broad interpretation of the commerce clause provided a constitutional justification for much of the social experimentation of the New Deal and after.

5

Outcomes

THE RESIGNATION OF THE CHIEF JUSTICE IN FEBRUARY 1930 MARKED THE end of the Taft court; the resignation of Justice Holmes in January 1932, marked the end of an era. With both men gone from the bench, it is time to look back over the work of the 1920s court, setting the stage for reviewing outcomes down through the 1930s. One of the most tumultuous decades in the history of the Supreme Court, sources of the tumult can be readily identified with rulings by Taft and Holmes. Such was the history of the Hughes court, Charles Evans Hughes having been nominated to replace Taft. Hughes, in turn, was followed by Harlan Fiske Stone in 1941. By then, the New Deal had recessed and World War II loomed. Meanwhile, changes in constitutional interpretations traceable back to Taft and Holmes had been largely absorbed.

On the domestic front, New Deal legislation appeared to point to a constitutional revolution. The commerce clause was to be the open door through which would pass highly unconventional legislation, the office and authority of the presidency, in the hands of Franklin Roosevelt, would be dramatically enhanced, and issues of free speech and civil liberties would receive increased attention in the press and from the public. Inasmuch as the Court of the 1930s down to 1937 was believed to be two-thirds conservative in judicial outlook, the prospect of a constitutional crisis of some kind was real. The crisis when it arose—and was surmounted by the "switch in time saves nine"—was not the product of revolution but of evolution, beginnings of which are traceable to opinions expressed, whether in the majority or in dissent, by members of the 1920s court, and chief among them, Taft and Holmes.

The very first intimations of an expansion of court approval of the lawmaking authority of Congress surfaced in two low-profile, somewhat related cases, *Railroad Commission of Wisconsin v. Chicago, Burlington and Quincy Railroad Company* and *Dayton-Goose Creek Railway v. United States*, both decided in 1922.[1] In these two cases, Taft's opinion for a unanimous Court though rather technical in character, anticipated the more significant judgments in the Stafford and Olsen rulings. In the Wisconsin Railroad Commission case, the Court affirmed the national authority to fix intrastate rail rates. As Taft stated, the Transportation Act of 1920 had as its chief purpose maintaining an adequate national rail system; therefore, under certain circumstances, intrastate rates could be affected. The second case coming under the 1920 act, *Dayton-Goose Creek*, involved the company's refusal to place in reserve all earnings above six percent, as required by the act. Taft's strongly worded opinion upholding the regulation was reminiscent of language found in *Munn v. Illinois*. The Chief pointed out that the law sought to "build up a system of railroads prepared to handle all interstate traffic of the country," that railroads were "dedicated to the public service," and that they were, in consequence, subject to a degree of regulation appropriate to their public character. These two decisions established firm precedents Taft was able to build on, leaving a fairly if not completely consistent advocacy of the uses of the commerce clause as might be required by changing business conditions.

Given Taft's record regarding the commerce clause as a regulatory provision of the Constitution (and bearing in mind his position in the Bailey child labor case), how would he have voted when it came to suits brought under the National Labor Relations Act of 1935? There seems to be little reason to doubt he would have joined the Court, or perhaps led it, in declaring the National Industrial Recovery Act bad law, as did a unanimous Court, or the First Agricultural Adjustment Act also rejected.[2] The question regarding Taft's position on the Wagner Act is in some ways an idle one because it takes him totally out of context. Yet, it is also a serious question because it would have put to the test "the ultimate logic" of the position Taft had already committed to in important cases.

Had he lived another ten years, Taft would have known the devastation of the Great Depression and the disillusionment of many Americans with free-wheeling capitalism. He may have looked with cautious approval on some of the early New Deal efforts, such as the Securities and Exchange Commission Act and the Glass-Steagall Act of 1933. After all, he had pushed hard for the postal savings bank system to help the small depositor. Nor would Taft, a sometime politician, have been indifferent to the results of the 1934 midterm elections and the 1936 Roosevelt landslide. On the other hand, his fear of too much democracy might have influenced his attitudes. And, most certainly FDR's proposal to reorganize the Supreme Court in the wake of his great political victory would have touched Taft's most tender spot. There is another element in Taft's large view of the place of the Supreme Court in American government. When he came on the Court as chief justice, his fear was that unless serious changes were made in the methods of its operation the institution might seem less and less relevant. For that reason, he had promoted the two Judges Acts. Had the risk of the charge of irrelevancy reappeared in a more dangerous way, he could have been moved to support key New Deal legislation. Nineteen thirty-six saw the court reject the Guffey Coal Act, designed to regulate labor-management relations in the coal industry, in *Carter v. Carter Coal Company* (1936).[3] Should the justices dismiss the National Labor Relations Act and/or the Social Security Act, talk about the "twilight of the Supreme Court" might become something more than a well-turned phrase. Taft would have moved mountains to stay the course of the sun, lest it set over the magnificent temple, the very essence of relevancy, that as chief justice he had caused to be built.

As interesting, even useful, as such speculation can be, it is more germane to recognize that without the spade work that Taft's commerce clause decisions had done, the Hughes court would have been on less firm constitutional ground in approving the relentless pursuit of reform by the New Deal. This, Hughes appeared to acknowledge in *National Labor Relations Board v. Jones and Laughlin Steel Company* (1937).[4] "We have frequently said that the legislative authority, exerted within the proper field, need not embrace all the evils within its reach. The Constitution does not forbid 'cautious advance, step by step' in dealing with evils which are exhibited in activities within the range of legislative power." Throughout Hughes's opinion he made it clear that Taft's decisions were much on his mind. His definition of "commerce," for example, is of a piece with Taft's understanding, expressed so well in the Stafford case. The opinion also reflects a concept of the national interests over those of the states. "The fundamental principle is that the power to regulate commerce . . . is a plenary power and may be exerted to protect interstate commerce 'no matter what the source of the dangers which threaten it'." Within a year's time, as the result of a series of decisions handed down, truck and bus drivers, tailors, cannery workers, electric generating plant employees, and newspaper editors had joined the steel workers under the umbrella of protection raised by the Wagner Act.[5] It was a triumph of the first magnitude for the New Deal, and William Howard Taft had a part in it.

No twentieth-century President, and possibly no President in the history of the office, exerted more power and influence than did Franklin Roosevelt. The cautious, somewhat discontinuous buildup of executive authority since the days of William McKinley reached high ground in the years 1933–1945. It may be too much to claim that William Howard Taft's conception of presidential power as expressed in his extra-Court writings and in his decision in *Myers v. United States* were parts of FDR's conscious thinking about the Oval Office. It *is* too much to insist that *Rathburn v. United States* diminished his power in any significant way.[6] What the Court's decision in that case did was reassert the principle of separation of powers. Nonetheless, Taft's *The President and His Powers*, along with the Myers opinion, convey the overall idea that the occupant of the White House possesses great political strength, as well as the freedom to go with it when conducting the diplomacy of the United States. Taft had rejected Theodore Roosevelt's "residuum of power" rule while insisting that the President should be free to make as much of the office as possible while remaining within boundaries established by the Constitution. Once the constitutionality of the National Labor Relations Act and the Social Security Act had been confirmed, FDR, increasingly turned his attention to foreign affairs, a preoccupation until the end of his life. With regard to Taft's place in all this, it must be said that, as chief justice, he had put no obstacles in FDR's path. When read in conjunction with his opinions under the commerce clause he had, wittingly or otherwise, contributed to Roosevelt's historical stature.

Few decisions revealed the sharply divergent thinking of Taft and Holmes on the issue of civil liberties than did the 1925 Gitlow case. The Chief wrote confidently that Gitlow's "Left Wing Manifesto" was incendiary and not protected by the Constitution. Holmes offered a provocative dissent: "Every idea is an incitement." In writing to Laski, however, he was more off-handed: "I let out a page of slack on the right of an ass to drool about proletarian dictatorship."[7] In the short run, Taft had his way, affirming "bad tendency," if not in so many words. In the long run, *Near v. Minnesota* (1931) tended to vindicate Holmes's understanding of freedom of speech when a state attempts to reduce or restrict it.[8] In the aftermath of World War I, Minnesota had passed a "gag" law. It provided for padlocking by injunction a newspaper for having published scandalous, malicious, defamatory, or obscene matter. The padlock could be lifted if the judge issuing the injunction was convinced by the publisher that no such material would again be put into print. What this amounted to was a form of prepublication censorship enforceable by a contempt of court citation. In a lengthy and carefully reasoned opinion for the majority, Chief Justice Hughes ruled the law of Minnesota an infringement of the liberty of the press guaranteed by the Fourteenth Amendment: "The state had enforced an unconstitutional restraint on publication." *Near v. Minnesota* was the first time in which a state law was held, by reason of its general character, to deprive persons of liberty without due process of law.[9] In consequence, important civil liberties had begun to be nationalized against state interference.

Civil liberties issues would gain increasing prominence during the sessions of the 1930s Court, especially when it came to denial of basic procedural rights for black citizens. Indeed, civil liberties began to take on a wider meaning as civil rights. This expansion touched on equal educational opportunities for blacks in *Missouri ex rel Gaines v. Canada* (1938).[10] But, for Justice Holmes, it was the failure of the states to safeguard the civil liberties of those accused and found guilty of heinous crimes that must be associated with his name. The landmark case was *Moore v. Dempsey* in 1922.[11] Five men of African descent had been tried and found guilty by an Arkansas court for the murder of a white man. For a nearly unanimous court, Holmes delivered a blistering indictment of Arkansas justice. Here is his description of the trial.

> Petitioners were brought into Court, informed that a certain lawyer was appointed their counsel and were placed on trial before a white jury—blacks being systemically excluded from both grand and petit juries. The Court and neighborhood were thronged with an adverse crowd that threatened the most dangerous consequences to anyone interfering with the desired result. The counsel did not venture to demand delay or a change of venue, to challenge a juryman or to ask for separate trials. He had no preliminary consultation with the accused, called no witnesses for the defence although they could be produced, and did not put the defendants on the stand. The trial lasted about three-quarters of an hour and in less than five minutes the jury brought in a verdict of guilty of murder in the first degree.

Holmes's conclusion followed from this description. "But if the case is that the whole proceeding is a mask—that counsel, jury and judge were swept to the fatal end by an irresistible wave of public passion, and that the State Courts failed to correct the wrong, neither perfection in the machinery for correction nor the possibility that the trial court and counsel saw no other way of avoiding an immediate outbreak of the mob, can prevent this Court from securing to the petitioners their constitutional rights." The language employed conveyed the outrage of all the justices except McReynolds.

Almost ten years elapsed before *Powell v. Alabama* (1932), the first "Scottsboro Case," came before the Supreme Court.[12] Seven black men had been convicted in a local court of the crime of rape and had been sentenced to die. The High Court ruled that, because no adequate counsel had been provided, their civil liberties, as mandated by the Fourteenth Amendment, had been expressly violated. The Court was guided, if not inspired, by Holmes's arguments in *Moore v. Dempsey*. The second "Scottsboro Case," *Norris v. Alabama* (1935), as mandated by the Fourteenth Amendment, confirmed the earlier opinion.[13] Testimony to the effect that no black person had served on either a grand or petit jury within living memory "made out a *prima facie* case of the denial of the equal protection which the Constitution guarantees." The very next year a case similar in nature was on the Court docket: *Brown v. Mississippi* (1936).[14] As mandated by the Fourteenth Amendment, three black men were convicted of murder solely on the strength of confessions obtained by brutal treatment. The Court called the confessions "spurious" and the trial a legal "farce." Such evidence was obviously inadmissible, so their convictions were set aside, the men having been denied process in its most elemental sense.

The Taft-Holmes relationship in matters judicial was virtually singular in character in the Adkins case. It will be recalled that the two justices dissented from a Court ruling that Congress had no constitutional authority to regulate wages for women working in the District of Columbia. What made the case exceptional was the basis for their dissents. In their separate opinions there was ample evidence of their belief that the law and society should meet and mix in a positive way, that the more vulnerable in society were due protections which fell within provisions of the Constitution. In their individual, but distinct, arguments Taft matched Holmes stride for stride. Fifteen years later the bread they had cast upon the waters returned with the adjudication of *West Coast Hotel Company v. Parrish* (1937).[15] As mandated by the Fourteenth Amendment, the State of Washington had enacted legislation making it unlawful to employ women and minors in any industry or occupation under conditions detrimental to their health or morals. It further required that wages be sufficient to the workers' maintenance. In a five-to-four decision, the Court upheld the Washington law. Chief Justice Hughes spoke for the majority, and in such vein as to make a direct connection with reasoning of Taft and Holmes in Adkins. "The Constitution does not recognize absolute and uncontrollable liberty [or contract]. The Liberty safe-guarded [by the Constitution] is liberty in a social organization which requires the protection of law against the evils which menace the health, safety, morals and welfare of the people." Further, "It is manifest that the established principles peculiarly applicable to the employment of women in whose protection the state has a special interest." "Even if the wisdom of the policy be regarded as debatable and its effects uncertain the state legislature is entitled to its judgment."

The Taft and Hughes courts had much more than a sequential relationship. In two important areas of constitutional law—namely, the use of the commerce clause to govern an ever more complex socioeconomy and a guarantee of civil liberties for all Americans—its influence helped direct the workings of the 1930s Court. Taft and Holmes, despite entertaining diverse views of the Constitution, had combined to help render the Supreme Court more relevant and therefore a more recognizably vital part of American government. Endowed with great gifts of mind and spirit, they used them wisely and well for their country, to which each man, in his own way, was utterly devoted.

Notes

INTRODUCTION

1. Irving H. Bartlett, *The American Mind at Mid-Nineteenth Century* (New York: Thomas Crowell, 1967), 13; William G. McLoughlin, *Modern Revivalism* (New York: Ronald Press, 1959), 24.

2. Henry F. May, *The Enlightenment in America* (Oxford: Oxford University Press, 1978); 3–149 cover the period 1688–1789.

3. Esmond Wright, *An Empire for Liberty* (Oxford: Basil Blackwell, 1995), 365.

4. James McCosh, *Realistic Philosophy*, 2 vols. (New York: Scribners, 1890), I:4.

5. Jefferson to George Washington, 4 December 1788, *Jefferson's Works*, Memorial Edition, 12 vols. (New York: G.P. Putnam's Sons, 1900), VII:223.

6. Victor Hugo Paltsist, *Washington's Farewell Address* (New York: Arno Press, 1935), 147.

7. Abraham Lincoln, *The Writings of Abraham Lincoln*, Constitutional Edition, 8 vols. (New York: G.P. Putnam's Sons, 1927), V:256.

8. Joseph Story, *Commentaries on the Constitution of the United States*, 2 vols. (Boston: Charles Little & James Brown, 1851), II:617.

9. Stow Persons, *American Minds* (New York: Henry Holt, 1958), 196–97.

CHAPTER 1. FELLOW NEW ENGLANDERS

1. Books dealing with the life of William Howard Taft—and, more particularly, with his life in the law—are not numerous but are generally of high quality. Henry F. Pringle, *The Life and Times of William Howard Taft*, 2 vols., (New York: Farrar and Rinehart, 1939) is a comprehensive account, based on a wide reading in the Taft *Papers*; it is, however, disappointing in its treatment of Taft as Chief Justice. In this latter respect much the best study is Alpheus Thomas Mason, *William Howard Taft: Chief Justice*, (New York: Simon and Schuster, 1964). Even so, Mason's account is marred by something of an animus regarding its subject. A more recent, brief biography is David H. Burton, *William Howard Taft In the Public Service*, (Malabar, Florida: Krieger Publishing Company, 1986). One older book also deserves mention: Allen E. Ragan, *Chief Justice Taft*, (Columbus, Ohio: Ohio Historical Society, 1938). Two worthwhile books on Taft's presidency are Donald F. Anderson, *A Conservative's Conception of the Presidency*, (Ithaca, N.Y.: Cornell University Press, 1968) and Paolo Coletta, *The Presidency of William Howard Taft*, (Lawrence, Kansas: University of Kansas Press, 1973). Finally, studies pertinent to understanding the total Taft as a public man include: Ralph E. Minger, *William Howard Taft and United States Diplomacy: The Apprenticeship Years, 1900–1908*, (Urbana, Ill.: University of Illinois Press, 1975) and Walter V. and Marie V. Scholes, *The Foreign Policies of the Taft Administration*, (Columbia, Mo.: University of Missouri Press, 1970).

2. Oliver Wendell Holmes, Jr., *Speeches*, (Boston: Little, Brown and Company, 1913), 21.

3. *Heard v. Sturgis*, 146 Mass. 545 (1888).

4. Any listing of books dealing with Holmes, the jurist, needs to be selective—such is the extent of the Holmes canon. Max Lerner's *The Mind and Faith of Justice Holmes*, (Boston: Little Brown and Co., 1943) is a brilliant compendium and a pioneering work. Three recent major biographies tend to outstrip and outshine earlier treatments. Sheldon N. Novick, *Honorable Justice*, (Boston: Little Brown and Co., 1989) while excellent, perhaps gives too little attention to Holmes and the law. Liva Baker, *The Justice From Beacon Hill*, (New York: Harper Collins, 1991) is well informed but somewhat speculative in spots. G. Edward White, *Justice Oliver Wendell Holmes Law and the Inner Self*, (New York: Oxford University Press, 1993) is strong in every respect and especially so in its analyses of Holmes and the law. It is more critical and argumentative than are Novick and Baker, and the better for it. A brief, scholarly study by Gary J. Aichele, *Oliver Wendell Holmes, Jr.: Scholar, Soldier, Judge*, (New York: Twayne, 1989) should not be overlooked. The two volumes by Mark DeW. Howe, *Oliver Wendell Holmes, The Shaping Years, 1841–1870*, (Cambridge: Harvard University Press, 1957) and *The Proving Years: 1870–1882*, (Harvard University Press, 1963) are indispensable for understanding the young Holmes. Two more focused books may round off what is a restricted summary of the literature. H.L. Pohlman, *Justice Oliver Wendell Holmes and Utilitarian Jurisprudence*, (Cambridge: Harvard University Press, 1984) and by the same author: *Justice Oliver Wendell Holmes, Free Speech and the Living Constitution*, (Cambridge: Harvard University Press, 1993).

5. Taft's heritage is well rehearsed in Pringle, *The Life and Times of William Howard Taft*, I:7–11.

6. Quoted in Frederick Flechter, Jr., "The Preparation of an American Aristocrat," *The New England Quarterly*, VI; 1, March, 1933, 9.

7. Quoted in Pringle, *Taft*, I:45.

8. Holmes to Canon Patrick Augustine Sheehan, July 17, 1909, *Holmes-Sheehan Correspondence*, Revised Edition, David H. Burton, ed., (Bronx, N.Y.: Fordham University Press, 1993).

9. Mark A. deWolfe Howe, *Oliver Wendell Holmes, The Shaping Years*, 62.

10. Pringle, *Taft*, I:34.

11. Holmes at Harvard is thoroughly discussed in Howe, *The Shaping Years*, 35–79.

12. Holmes, *Touched With Fire*, (Cambridge: Harvard University Press, 1943), conveys via letters and diary entries Holmes's experiences of the horrors of war.

13. Holmes, "Memorial Day Address," in Max Lerner, ed., *The Mind and Faith of Justice Holmes*, 9–16; esp. 13.

14. John Wise, "A Vindication of the Government of New England Churches" in Edmund S. Morgan, editor, *Puritan Political Ideas*, (Indianapolis: Bobbs Merrill, 1965), 251–267, 262–63.

15. Elisha Williams, "The Essential Rights and Liberties of Protestants," Morgan, *Puritan Political Ideas*, 268–304, 269–70.

16. Jonathan Mayhew, "A Discourse Concerning Unlimited Submission and Non-Resistance to the Higher Powers," Morgan, *Puritan Political Ideas*, ed. Edmund S. Morgan (Indianapolis: Bobbs Merrill, 1965), 305–330, 313; 330.

17. Abraham Williams, "A Sermon Preached at Boston" [for Election Day] Morgan, *Puritan Political Ideas*, ed. Edmund S. Morgan (Indianapolis: Bobbs Merrill, 1965), 331–352.

18. Samuel Langdon, "Government Corrupted by Vice and Recovered by Righteousness," Morgan, *Puritan Political Ideas*, ed. Edmund S. Morgan (Indianapolis: Bobbs Merrill, 1965), 351–372, esp. 358; 361.

19. Ezra Stiles, "A History of Three of the Judges of King CharlesI," Morgan, *Puritan*

Political Ideas, ed. Edmund S. Morgan (Indianapolis: Bobbs Merrill, 1965), 373–392, esp. 373; 375.

20. Andre Siegfried, *America Comes of Age*, (New York: Harcourt Brace, 1927), 34.

21. James Bryce, *The American Commonwealth*, 2 vols., (New York: MacMillan and Company, 1895), I:306.

CHAPTER 2. THE TIMES AND THE JUDGES

1. Merle Curti, *The Growth of American Thought*, (New York: Harper & Row, 1964), 517.

2. G. Edward White, *The American Judicial Tradition*, (New York: Oxford University Press, 1976), 157–160; 180–181.

3. Richard Hofstadter, *Social Darwinism in American Thought*, (Boston: Beacon Press, 1969), 31.

4. John Winthrop, "A Lecture on Earthquakes," (Boston, 1755) in Max Savelle, editor, *The Colonial Origins of American Thought*, (New York: Van Nostrand, 1964), 133–34.

5. Henry Ward Beecher, *Evolution and Religion*, (New York: Ford, Howard and Hilbert, 1885), 45–46.

6. Andrew Carnegie, "Wealth," *North American Review*, CXLVIII (June, 1889), 654–55.

7. William Graham Sumner, "The Absurd Effort To Make The World Over," *War and Other Essays*, Albert G. Keller, ed., (New Haven: Yale University Press, 1911), 195–210.

8. William Graham Sumner, *Earth Hunger*, (New Haven: Yale University Press, 1934), 31.

9. William Howard Taft, "The Right to Private Property," *Michigan Law Journal*, III, 8, August 1894, 215–233; Taft, "Recent Criticism of the Federal Judiciary," *Present Day Problems*, (Freeport, N.Y.: Books For Libraries Press, 1967), 290–332.

10. Taft, "Labor and Capital," *Present Day Problems*, 241–272.

11. Norman Pollack, *Populist Response to Industrial America*, (New York: Harcourt Brace, 1962), 21.

12. *Moores & Co.* v. *Bricklayers Union No. 1 W.H. Stephenson, P.H. McElroy et al.* 45 Federal Reporter 730–745.

13. Lincoln Caplan, *The Tenth Justice The Solicitor General and the Rule of Law*, (New York: Knopf, 1987), 5.

14. Bering Sea Case, Pringle, *Taft*, I, 116–118.

15. Toledo, *Ann Arbor and Northern Michigan Railway Co.* v. *Brotherhood of Locomotive Engineers* 54 Federal Reporter 710.

16. *In Re: Phelan* 62 Federal Reporter 802–823.

17. *Ibid.*

18. *Voight Case* 79 Federal Reporter 561.

19. *Narramore Case* 96 Federal Reporter 926.

20. *Addystone Pipe and Steel Co. Case* 85 Federal Reporter 271.

21. Taft, "The Right of Private Property," *Michigan Law Journal* III:8 (August 1894): 215–33.

22. Taft, "Recent Criticism of the Federal Judiciary," in *Present Day Problems* (Freeport, N.Y.: Books for Libraries Press, 1967).

23. Oliver Wendell Holmes, Jr., *The Common Law*, (Boston: Little Brown and Company, 1881), edition cited, 1963.

24. Holmes to William James, April 19, 1868, quoted in White, *Holmes*, 94.

25. Holmes, *The Common Law*, 5.
26. Holmes, *The Common Law*, 6–34.
27. Holmes, *The Common Law*, 35–62.
28. Holmes, *The Common Law*, 63–103.
29. Holmes, *The Common Law*, 227–240.
30. 170 Mass. 596.
31. 177 Mass. 485.
32. 134 Mass. 449–50.
33. 138 Mass. 175–76.
34. 150 Mass. 194.
35. 163 Mass. 117, 123.
36. 167 Mass. 92,104.
37. 170 Mass. 492, 504.
38. Holmes, "The Path of the Law," *Harvard Law Review*, X (1896), 457–478.
39. Holmes, "Law in Science and Science in Law," *Collected Legal Papers*, (New York: Peter Smith, 1952), 210–243.
40. Holmes, "Learnng and Science," *Collected Legal Papers*, 138–140.

Chapter 3. Capital Men

1. Pringle, *Taft*, I:167–210.
2. Ralph E. Minger, *William Howard Taft and United States Foreign Policy: The Apprenticeship Years 1900–1908*, (Urbana: University of Illinois Press, 1975), 34–36.
3. Pringle, *Taft*, I:216–219.
4. Minger, *Taft*, 74–77.
5. *Ibid*, 136.
6. Taft, *Four Aspects of Civil Virtue*, (New York: Charles Scribner's Sons, 1907).
7. *Ibid*.
8. Pringle, *Taft*, I:305–310.
9. Taft, "Labor and Capital," in *Present Day Problems*, (Freeport: N.Y.: Books for Libraries Press, 1967), 241–272.
10. Taft to W.R.Nelson, February 22, 1909, quoted in Pringle, *Taft*, I:381–83.
11. George E. Mowry, *The Era of Theodore Roosevelt*, (New York: Harper Brothers, 1958), 288–291.
12. Taft to Archie Butt, quoted in Archibald Willingham Butt, *Taft and Roosevelt: The Intimate Letters of Archie Butt*, 2 vols., (Garden City, N.Y.: Doubleday, Doran and Company, 1930), II:635.
13. Pringle, *Taft*, II:737.
14. Taft, *Popular Government*, (New Haven: Yale University Press, 1913).
15. Taft, *The Anti-Trust Act and the Supreme Court*, (New York: Harper and Row, 1914).
16. Taft, *The President And His Powers*, (New York: Columbia University Press, 1924).
17. Valerie Conner, *The National War Labor Board*, (Chapel Hill, N.C.: University of North Carolina Press, 1983).
18. Taft, *Liberty Under Law*, (New Haven: Yale University Press, 1922).
19. Holmes to Pollock, December 21, 1902, *Holmes-Pollock Lettes*, 2 vols., ed. Mark Howe (Cambridge, Mass.: Harvard University Press, 1941), I, 109.
20. Holmes, John Marshall, *Collected Legal Papers*, 266–271; esp. 269.
21. David H. Burton, *Oliver Wendell Holmes, Jr.*, (Boston: Twayne Publishers, 1980), 135–146.

22. *Otis v. Parker* 187 U.S. 606 (1903).
23. *Northern Securities Case* 193 U.S. 197 (1904).
24. *Lochner v. New York* 198 U.S. 45 (1905).
25. *Swift and Co. v. United States* 196 U.S. 375 (1905).
26. *Missouri v. Illinois* 252 U.S. 416 (1905).
27. *Haddock v. Haddock* 201 U.S. 562, 638 (1905).
28. *Carroll v. Greenwich Insurance Co.* 199 U.S. 401 (1903).
29. *Ellis v. United States* 206 U.S. 246 (1906).
30. *Adair v. United States* 208 U.S. 161 (1906); *First Employers' Liability Cases* 207 U.S. 463, 571 (1908).
31. *Second Employers' Liability Cases* 223 U.S. 1 (1912).
32. *Keller v. United States* 213 U.S. 138, 149 (1908).
33. *Hoke v. United States* 227 U.S. 138 (1913).
34. *Pullman v. Kansas* 216 U.S. 56, 75 (1909).
35. *Kuhn v. Fairmont Coal Co.* 215 U.S. 349, 370 (1909).
36. *ICC v. Illinois Central Railway Co.* 215 U.S. 462 (1910); *ICC v. Chicago, Rock Island, and Pacific Ry. Co.* 218 U.S. 88 (1910).
37. *Standard Oil Co. v. United States* 221 U.S. 1 (1911); *American Tobacco v. United States* 221 U.S. 106 (1911); *Hipolite Egg Co. v United States* 220 U.S. 45 (1911).
38. *United States v. Winslow* 227 U.S. 202 (1913).
39. *Dr. Miles Medical Co. v. Park and Sons Co.* 220 U.S. 373, 409 (1911).
40. *Noble State Banks v. Haskell* 219 U.S. 105 (1911).
41. *Cedar Rapids Gas Co. v. Cedar Rapids* 223 U.S. 655 (1911).
42. *Minnesota Rate Cases* 230 U.S. 350 (1913).
43. *Nash v. United States* 229 U.S. 373 (1912).
44. *International Harvester Co. v. Kentucky* 234 U.S. 216 (1914).
45. *Gompers v. United States* 233 U.S. 604 (1913).
46. *Lawlor v. Leowe* 235 U.S. 522 (1914).
47. Brandeis to Thomas Watt Gregory, April 14, 1916, *Letters of Louis D. Brandeis,* Melvin I. Uroksky and David W. Levy, eds., 5 vols., (Albany, N.Y.: State University of New York Press, 1971), IV:65.
48. Brandeis to Holmes, December 9, 1882, *Brandeis Letters,* I:65.
49. Brandeis to Holmes, September 3, 1902, *Brandeis Letters,* I:206–07.
50. *Muller v. Oregon* 208 U.S. 412 (1908).
51. Holmes to Laski, March 1, 1925, *Laski Letters,* I:485.
52. *Southern Pacific Railway Co. v. Jensen* 244 U.S. 205, 218 (1916).
53. *Hammer v. Dagenhart* 247 U.S. 251, 277 (1917).
54. *Wilson v. New* 243 U.S. 332 (1917).
55. Wilfred E. Rumble, *American Legal Realism,* (Ithaca, N.Y.: Cornell University Press, 1968), 41–44. Jerome Frank, "Are Judges Human? Part One: The Effect of Legal Thinking on the Assumption that Judges Behave Like Human Beings," University of Pennsylvania *Law Review,* vol. 80, 17ff. Roscoe Pound, "Fifty Years of Jurisprudence: IV Realist Schools, *Harvard Law Review,* vol. 51, 777ff.
56. Holmes to Pollock, August 30, 1914, *Holmes-Pollock Letters,* I:219; Holmes to Pollock, November 7, 1914, *Holmes-Pollock Letters,* I:222.
57. Holmes to Lewis Einstein, Oct. 12, 1914, *Holmes-Einstein Letters,* James B. Peabody, ed., (London: MacMillan, 1964), 100.
58. Holmes to Pollock, November 3, 1917, *Holmes-Pollock Letters,* I:250.
59. *Selective Service Draft Cases* 245 U.S. 366 (1918); *Northern Pacific Railroad Co. v. North Dakota* 250 U.S. 135 (1923).
60. *Schenck v. United States* 249 U.S. 47 (1919).
61. Holmes to Laski, February 28, 1919, *Holmes-Laski Letters,* I:186.

62. *Frowerk* v. *United States* 240 U.S. 211 (1918).
63. *Debs* v. *United States* 249 U.S. 204 (1918).
64. Holmes to Laski, March 12, 1919, *Holmes-Laski Letters*, I:190.
65. *Abrams* v. *United States* 250 U.S. 616, 624 (1919).
66. Holmes to Pollock, December 14, 1919, *Holmes-Pollock Letters*, II:32.
67. *Abrams* v. *United States*, 250 U.S. 616 (1919).
68. Holmes to Pollock, Oct. 16, 1919, *Holmes-Pollock Letters*, II:29.

CHAPTER 4. THE 1920s COURT

1. Alpheus Thomas Mason, *William Howard Taft: Chief Justice* (New York: Simon & Schuster, 1964), 89–90.
2. Henry F. Pringle, *The Life and Times of William Howard Taft*, 2 vols. (New York: Farrar and Rinehard, 1939), 960–972.
3. G. Edward White, *The American Judicial Tradition*, (New York: Oxford University Press, 1976), 203–4.
4. Taft, "First Annual Message," *Presidential Addresses and State*, (New York: Doubleday, 1910), 477.
5. Taft, "Address at Charlotte, N.C.," May 20, 1909, *ibid*, 104–116; esp. 108.
6. Taft, "The Attack on the Courts and Legal Procedure," *Kentucky Law Review*, 5:2 (November 1916), 3–24; esp. 14.
7. Taft, "Adequate Machinery For Judicial Business," *American Bar Association Journal*, 7 (September 1921), 453–4; esp. 454.
8. Taft, "Three Needed Steps of Progress," *American Bar Association Journal*, 8 (January 1922), 34–6.
9. Mason, *Taft*, 99.
10. *Congressional Record*, 67th Congress, 2nd sess. 5113–4.
11. *Congressional Record*, 67th Congress, 2nd sess. 4040.
12. *Congressional Record*, 67th Congress, 2nd sess. 4064.
13. *Congressional Record*, 67th Congress, 2nd sess. 6407.
14. *Congressional Record*, 67th Congress, 2nd sess. 4843.
15. Taft, "Possible and Needed Reforms in the Administration of Justice in Federal Courts," *American Bar Association Journal*, 8 (September 1922).
16. *Congressional Record*, 67th Congress, 2nd sess. 8547.
17. Allen E. Ragan, *Chief Justice Taft* (Columbus: Ohio Historical Society, 1938), 112–13.
18. Mason, *Taft*, 200 nn. 46, 48.
19. Holmes, "Natural Law," *Collected Legal Papers*, (New York: Peter Smith, 1952), 310–316.
20. Holmes to Harold J. Laski, 27 May 1921, *Holmes-Laski Letters*, Mark Howe, editor, 2 volumes, (Cambridge: Harvard University Press, 1953), I:339.
21. Holmes to Laski, 12 July 1921, *ibid*.
22. Holmes to Sir Frederick Pollock, 11 July 1921, *Holmes-Pollock Letters*, II:72.
23. Holmes to Pollock, 2 October 1921, *Holmes-Pollock Letters*, II:79.
24. Holmes to Pollock, 21 May 1922, *Holmes-Pollock Letters*, II:96.
25. Holmes to Pollock, 18 September 1927, *Holmes-Pollock Letters*, II:205.
26. Holmes to Laski, 30 October 1921, I:377; to Laski, May 3, 1922, *Holmes-Laski Letters*, I:423.
27. Holmes to Laski, 5 May 1922, *Holmes-Pollock Letters*, I:422.
28. Holmes to Pollock, 27 April 1919, *Holmes-Pollock Letters*, II:1.
29. Holmes to Pollock, 26 May 1919, *Holmes-Pollock Letters*, II:13.

30. Holmes to Laski, 18 May 1919, *Holmes-Laski Letters*, I:204–05.
31. Holmes to Pollock, 17 June 1919, *Holmes-Pollock Letters*, II:15.
32. Holmes to Pollock, 14 December 1919, *Holmes-Pollock Letters*, II:32.
33. Holmes to Pollock, 23 January 1921, *Holmes-Pollock Letters*, II:87.
34. Holmes to Laski, 21 September 1921, *Holmes-Laski Letters*, I:372.
35. Holmes to Pollock, 11 July 1921, *Holmes-Pollock Letters*.
36. Holmes to Learned Hand, 3 March 1923, quoted in Mason, *Taft*, 199.
37. Holmes to Pollock, 21 May 1922, *Holmes-Pollock Letters*, I:96.
38. Holmes to Taft, 10 February 1930, quoted in Pringle, *Taft*, II:1079.
39. Taft to Gus Karger, 31 January 1916, quoted in Mason, *Taft*, 72.
40. Mason, *Brandeis A Free Man's Life*, (New York: Viking Press, 1941), 489.
41. Brandeis to Alice Goldmark Brandeis, Dec. 4, 1918, *Letters of Louis D. Brandeis*, editors, Melvin Urofsky and David Levy, 5 vols, (Albany: Press of State University of New York, 1971–1978), IV:370.
42. Taft to Brandeis, 24 July 1921 and 19 August 1921, in Mason, *Brandeis*, 538.
43. Brandeis to Felix Frankfurter, quoted in Mason, *Taft*, 201.
44. Taft to Helen Taft Manning, 11 June 1923, Mason, *Brandeis*, 538.
45. Taft to Horace Taft, 28 November 1925, White, *Holmes*, 319.
46. *American Steel Foundries v. Tri-City* 257 U.S. 184 (1921).
47. *United Mine Workers v. Coronado Coal Co.* 359 U.S. 344 (1922).
48. *Gitlow v. New York* 268 U.S. 652 (1925).
49. *Schwimmer v. United States* 279 U.S. 644 (1929).
50. Holmes to Laski, 23 August 1929, *Holmes-Laski Letters*, II:117.
51. *Truax v. Corrigan* 247 U.S. 312 (1921).
52. *Stafford v. Wallace* 258 U.S. 495 (1922); *Board of Trade of the City of Chicago v. Olsen* 262 U.S. 01 (1922); *Bailey v. Drexel Furniture Co.* 259 U.S. 20 (1922).
53. *Olmstead v. United States* 277 U.S. 438 (1928).
54. *Adkins v. Children's Hospital* 261 U.S. 525 (1923).
55. *Penna. Coal Co. v. Mahon* 260 U.S. 393 (1922); *United Zinc Co. v. Britt* 258 U.S. 268 (1922); *Bartels v. Iowa* 262 U.S. 404 (1923).
56. Holmes to Pollock, 31 December 1922, *Holmes-Pollock Letters*, II:109.
57. Holmes to Laski, 13 January 1922, *Holmes-Laski Letters*, I:473.
58. Holmes to Pollock, 29 March 1922, *Holmes-Pollock Letters*, II:92.
59. *United Zinc Co. v. Britt* 258 U.S. 268 (1922).
60. *Meyers v. Nebraska* 262 U.S. 390 (1923).
61. *Bartels v. Iowa* 262 U.S. 404 (1923).
62. *Myers v. United States* 272 U.S. 52 (1926); *Ex parte Grossman* 267 U.S. 87 (1925).
63. *Leach v. Carlile* 258 U.S. 138, 140 (1921).
64. *United States v. Sullivan* 278 U.S. 259 (1926).
65. *Nixon v. Herndon* 273 U.S. 536 (1922).
66. *Buck v. Bell* 274 U.S. 200 (1927); *Olmstead v. United States* 277 U.S. 438 (1927).
67. Novick, *Holmes*, 261.
68. Mason, *Taft*, 261.
69. Holmes to Sheehan, 5 July 1912, *Holmes-Sheehan Correspondence*, 64.
70. Holmes to Dr. John Wu, 21 July 1925, *Justice Holmes to Dr. Wu An Intimate Correspondence, 1921–1932*, (New York: Cardinal Book Co., n.d.), 31.
71. Holmes, *The Common Law*, 7.
72. Ibid.

CHAPTER 5. OUTCOMES

1. *Railroad Commission of Wisconsin v. Chicago, Burlington and Quincy Railroad Co.* 257 U.S. 563 (1922); *Dayton-Goose Creek Railway v. United States* 263 U.S. 456 (1924).

2. *Schechter* v. *United States* 295 U.S. 495 (1935); *United States* v. *Butler* 297 U.S. 1 (1936).

3. *Carter* v. *Carter Coal Co.* 198 U.S. 238 (1936).

4. *National Labor Relations Board* v. *Jones and Laughlin Steel Co.* 301 U.S. I (1937).

5. Stanley I. Kutler, "Chief Justice Taft, National Regulation, and the Commerce Power," *The Journal of American History*, 51, 1964–1965, 651–668, gives an in-depth and telling analysis of the subject.

6. *Rathbun* v. *United States* 295 U.S. 602 (1935).

7. Holmes to Laski, 24 June 1925, *Holmes-Laski Letters*, I:752.

8. *Near* v. *Minnesota* 283 U.S. 697 (1931).

9. Robert E. Cushman, Leading Constitutional Decisions, (New York: Appleton, Century Crofts, Inc., 1955), 113.

10. *Missouri ex rel Gaines* v. *Canada* 305 U.S. 337 (1938).

11. *Moore* v. *Dempsey* 261 U.S. 86 (1923).

12. *Powell* v. *Alabama* 287 U.S. 45 (1932).

13. *Norris* v. *Alabama* 294 U.S. 587 (1935).

14. *Brown* v. *Mississippi* 297 U.S. 278 (1936).

15. *West Coast Hotel Co.* v. *Parrish* 300 U.S. 379 (1937).

Bibliography

Aichele, Gary J. *Oliver Wendell Holmes, Jr.: Scholar, Soldier, Judge.* New York: Twayne, 1989.

Anderson, Donald F. *A Conservative's Conception of the Presidency.* Ithaca, N.Y.: Cornell University Press, 1968.

Baker, Liva *The Justice from Beacon Hill.* New York: Harper Collins, 1991.

Bartlett, Irving H. *The American Mind at Mid-Nineteenth Century.* New York: Thomas Crowell, 1967.

Beecher, Henry Ward. *Evolution and Religion.* New York: Ford, Howard and Hilbert, 1885.

Bryce, James. *The American Commonwealth.* 2 vols. New York: Macmillan and Company, 1895.

Burton, David H. *Political Ideas of Justice Holmes.* Madison, N.J.: Fairleigh Dickenson University Press, 1993.

————. *Oliver Wendell Holmes, Jr.* Boston: Twayne Publishers, 1980.

————. *William Howard Taft in the Public Service.* Malabar, Fl.: Krieger Publishing Company, 1986.

Butt, Archibald Willingham. *Taft and Roosevelt: The Intimate Letters of Archie Butt.* 2 vols. Garden City, N.Y.: Doubleday, Doran and Company, 1930.

Caplan, Lincoln. *The Tenth Justice: The Solicitor General and the Rule of Law.* New York: Knopf, 1987.

Coletta, Paola. *The Presidency of William Howard Taft.* Lawrence: University of Kansas Press, 1973.

Conner, Valerie. *The National War Labor Board.* Chapel Hill: University of North Carolina Press, 1983.

Curti, Merle. *The Growth of American Thought.* New York: Harper & Row, 1964.

Cushman, Robert E. *Leading Constitutional Decisions.* New York: Appleton, Century Crofts, 1955.

Duffy, Herbert S. *William Howard Taft.* New York: Minton, Balch and Co., 1930.

Hofstadter, Richard. *Social Darwinism in American Thought.* Boston: Beacon Press, 1969.

Holmes, Oliver Wendell Jr. *Collected Legal Papers.* New York: Peter Smith, 1952.

————. *Holmes-Laski Letters,* ed., Mark Howe. 2 vols. Cambridge, Mass.: Harvard University Press, 1953.

————. *Holmes-Pollock Letters,* ed. Mark Howe, 2 vols. Cambridge, Mass.: Harvard University Press, 1941.

————. *Holmes-Einstein Letters,* ed. James B. Peabody. London: Macmillan, 1964.

————. *Holmes-Sheehan Correspondence.* ed. David H. Burton, rev. edition Bronx, N.Y.: Fordham University Press, 1993.

———. *Holmes to Dr. Wu: An Intimate Correspondence, 1921–1932*. New York: Cardinal Book Co., n.d..

———. *Speeches*. Boston: Little, Brown and Company, 1913.

———. *Touched with Fire*. ed. Mark Howe, Cambridge, Mass.: Harvard University Press, 1943.

Howe, Mark DeW. *Oliver Wendell Holmes, Jr.: The Shaping Years, 1841–1870*. Cambridge, Mass.: Harvard University Press, 1959.

———. *Oliver Wendell Holmes, Jr.: The Proving Years, 1870–1882*. Cambridge, Mass.: Harvard University Press, 1963.

Jefferson, Thomas. *Works*. Memorial Edition, 12 vols. New York: G. P. Putnam's Sons, 1906.

Lerner, Max, ed. *The Mind and Faith of Justice Holmes*. Boston: Little, Brown and Co., 1943.

Lincoln, Abraham. *The Writings of Abraham Lincoln*. Constitutional Edition, 8 vols. New York: G.P. Putnam's Sons, 1927.

Mason, Alpheus Thomas. *Brandeis: A Free Man's Life*. New York: Viking Press, 1941.

———. *William Howard Taft: Chief Justice*. New York: Simon and Schuster, 1964.

May, Henry F. *The Enlightenment in America*. Oxford: Oxford University Press, 1978.

McCosh, James. *Realistic Philosophy*. 2 vols. New York: Scribners, 1890.

Minger, Ralph E. *William Howard Taft and United States Diplomacy: The Apprenticeship Years*. 1900–1908. Urbana: University of Illinois Press, 1975.

Morgan, Edmund S., ed. *Puritan Political Ideas*. Indianapolis: Bobbs Merrill, 1965.

Mowry, George E. *The Era of Theodore Roosevelt*. New York: Harper Brothers, 1958.

Novick, Sheldon N. *Honorable Justice*. Boston: Little Brown and Co., 1989.

Paltsist, Victor Hugo *Washington's Farewell Address*. New York: Arno Press, 1935.

Persons, Stow. *American Minds*. New York: Henry Holt, 1958.

Pohlman, H. L. *Justice Oliver Wendell Holmes and Utilitarian Jurisprudence*. Cambridge, Mass.: Harvard University Press, 1984.

———. *Justice Oliver Wendell Holmes: Free Speech and the Living Constitution*. Cambridge, Mass.: Harvard University Press, 1993.

Pollack, Norman. *Populist Response to Industrial America*. New York: Harcourt Brace, 1962.

Pringle, Henry F. *The Life and Times of William Howard Taft*. 2 vols. New York: Farrar and Rinehart, 1939.

Ragan, Allen E. *Chief Justice Taft*. Columbus: Ohio Historical Society, 1938.

Rumble, Wilfred E. *American Legal Realism*. Ithaca, N.Y.: Cornell University Press, 1968.

Savelle, Max, ed. *The Colonial Origins of American Thought*. New York: Van Nostrand, 1964.

Scholes, Walter V. and Marie V. *The Foreign Policies of the Taft Administration*. Columbia: University of Missouri Press, 1970.

Siegfried, Andre. *America Comes of Age*. New York: Harcourt Brace, 1927.

Story, Joseph. *Commentaries on the Constitution of the United States*. 2 vols. Boston: Charles Little & James Brown, 1851.

Sumner, William Graham. *Earth Hunger*. New Haven: Yale University Press, 1934.

————. *War and Other Essays.* ed. Albert G. Keller. New Haven: Yale University Press, 1911.

Taft, William Howard. *Four Aspects of Civic Virtue.* New York: Charles Scribner's Sons, 1907.

————. *Liberty Under Law.* New Haven: Yale University Press, 1922.

————. *Popular Government.* New Haven: Yale University Press, 1913.

————. *Present Day Problems.* Freeport, N.Y.: Books For Libraries Press, 1967.

————. *The Anti-Trust Act and the Supreme Court.* New York: Harper and Row, 1914.

————. *The President and His Powers.* New York: Columbia University Press, 1924.

White, G. Edward. *The American Judicial Tradition.* New York: Oxford University Press, 1976.

————. *Justice Oliver Wendell Holmes Law and the Inner Self.* New York: Oxford University Press, 1993.

Wright, Esmond. *An Empire for Liberty.* Oxford: Basil Blackwell, 1995.

Index